Follow the Flock

ALSO BY SALLY COULTHARD

The Little Book of Building Fires
The Little Book of Snow
The Hedgehog Handbook
The Bee Bible

Follow
the Flock

How Sheep Shaped Human Civilization

SALLY COULTHARD

PEGASUS BOOKS
NEW YORK LONDON

FOLLOW THE FLOCK

Pegasus Books, Ltd.
148 West 37th Street, 13th Floor
New York, NY 10018

ISBN: 978-1-64313-658-5

10 9 8 7 6 5 4 3 2 1

Printed in the United States of America
Distributed by Simon & Schuster
www.pegasusbooks.com

For Maddy, Isabella and Emma

CONTENTS

1

How to Get a Sheep to Stand Still   1
*A man buried with a fox, a breastfed lamb and
the secrets of ancient wee*

2

Wool's Scaly Secret   17
*A 2,400-year-old woman frozen in time, fireproof
underpants and corsets for Roman soldiers*

3

Why Some Sheep are so Rooed   33
*A mummy's tattoos, the invention of scissors and
a ram on the run*

4

Tough as Old Boots   47
*Lactose intolerance, Cyclops the cheesemaker and
a sheep with two heads*

5

Rhymes and Ridiculous Cures   65

Bumfits, black sheep and the wrong star sign

6

Mr and Mrs Bo-Peep   85

Shepherd wanted, blasted sheep and the saving grace of crushed testicles

7

Dogs and Drovers   107

Come By, Corgis and the Bank of Black Sheep

8

Scouring and Spinning   127

Fairies, fleece grease and extra soft loo roll

9

Knit for Victory   147

The world's oldest socks, workhouses and how wool helped win the war

10

'Sheepe Hath Payed For It All'   175

Wool churches, white monks and the crime of owling

11

Sheep Devour People   195

Ghost ships, green cheese and 'Get off my land'

12

Spinning a Yarn   219

*Fisherman's jumpers, men in tights and a famous
execution*

13

Mills and Boom   237

*White slavery, wool-lined coffins and 'la maladie
de Bradford'*

14

Up, Up and Away   261

Bad science, sex and sheep in space

Notes   279

Index   295

I

HOW TO GET A SHEEP
TO STAND STILL

A man buried with a fox, a breastfed lamb
and the secrets of ancient wee

What have sheep ever done for us? On the face of it, they're just white noise in the countryside, slowly chewing the cud while we get on with our hurried lives. We sometimes notice them, come the Easter sweetness of spring-time lambs, but for most of the year they're invisible.

And yet, of any animal that has lived on this planet, sheep have shaped the course of human history. From Viking warriors to Renaissance painters, and from Iron Age sacrifices to the rolling hills and Bo-Peep imagery of 'Ye Olde England', sheep have been central to the human story. They've fed us, clothed us, changed our diet, made us both richer and poorer, altered our landscape, helped build great civilizations and win wars, decorated our homes, allowed us to create artistic treasures, and financed pioneers and privateers to conquer large swathes of the Earth. Vast fortunes have been built on the backs of sheep, and cities shaped by shepherds' markets and meat trading, but to begin the story we must travel back to the dawn of farming, that moment in time when our spear-throwing ancestors shifted from chasing and hunting prey to raising their own animals.

Between 10 and 20 million years ago, sheep's earliest ancestor evolved in the freezing mountains of Central Asia. During the last Ice Age, these tough, high-altitude creatures began to move outwards - some trotted westward, towards Europe, others eastward into Siberia. Some even made it as far as North America, crossing the frozen Bering Strait around 750,000 years ago.

The breed that gave us all modern domesticated sheep was the one that headed west - the 'Asiatic mouflon'; a dark-coloured, hairy beast with a soft, woolly undercoat. Unlike the sheep you find on today's farms, these archaic ovines had large horns and, instead of needing to be sheared, naturally moulted every year. The one thing they did have in common with modern sheep, however, is that they were delicious. From the moment our prehistoric ancestors clapped eyes on wild sheep, we consistently and energetically hunted them for food.

And then something happened. Around eleven thousand years ago hunter-gatherers turned their attention towards growing stuff. At a number of sites across a wide, curving area that has become known as the 'Fertile Crescent' - which stretches across the Middle East from Egypt through to the Persian Gulf - we find that people are starting to cultivate cereals and pulses and, crucially, rearing their own animals. Humans start to keep sheep.

Quite why they did this, we don't know. Maybe we over-hunted or over-exploited our wild resources. Perhaps the fluctuating climate allowed us to grow crops that previously wouldn't take. Maybe the way we organized ourselves socially changed, or population numbers increased, or we suddenly had an abundance of resources that allowed us the freedom to experiment with farming. It's a puzzle, but what is becoming clear from the archaeology is that different groups of people, totally unconnected, started tinkering with farming at around the same time.

One of the earliest places this happened was a small village in central Turkey. The site of Asikli Hoyuk had intrigued archaeologists for years and had long been suspected of being important in the story of farming. This hunch was proved right in 2014, when the bones of hundreds of different animals were discovered. A team led by zooarchaeologist Mary Stiner of the University of Arizona in Tucson uncovered archaeological layers filled with the rubbish and remains of human occupation between 10,500 and 9,500 years ago.

Sifting through the debris it became clear that what the villagers were eating over time had changed dramatically. For the first 500 years the men, women and children of the settlement feasted on wild fish, hares, tortoises, deer and a number of wild sheep. For the next 500 years, however, the proportion of ovine bones steadily rises until, by 9,500 years ago, nearly all the remains come from sheep.

Analysis of ancient sheep pee, which leaves behind salt traces, also showed how quickly sheep came to dominate the village;[1] over the relatively short thousand-year period that Asikli Hoyuk was occupied, people shifted from hunting wild sheep, to then keeping just a few tethered up in the narrow alleyways between the mud houses, to finally large-scale management of sheep in pens on the edge of the village. Sheep farming had arrived.

Although 'When?' is often the first question we ask about our switch from hunting and gathering to farming, the more interesting question is perhaps 'How?'. The relationship between sheep and humans isn't one of mutual symbiosis, the beautiful harmony that exists, say, between man and dog. Sheep don't need us, and yet we've somehow persuaded them to stay.

One idea is that the dog should take credit. In the wild, wolves have been seen herding caribou as part of their hunting strategy, and it's been suggested that an enterprising Stone Age individual saw this natural sheepdog instinct and used it to their own advantage. Perhaps our ancient ancestors realized that, with the help of a canine companion, wild sheep could be herded and managed without too much effort – turning a feral food resource into a controlled flock. It's true that people started to keep 'pets' some years before they started to domesticate livestock. One lovely example in northern Jordan – a 16,500-year-old grave at Uyun al-Hammam – uncovered a man deliberately buried with his red, presumably tame, fox,[2] but training a wild dog to round up wild sheep would have been chaotic, if not impossible. The days of *One Man and His Dog* were still some way off. If anything, as we'll see later in the book, sheep helped to domesticate dogs (see Chapter 7, page 109).

It's much easier to domesticate an animal if you can catch it young. Many theories about how sheep were domesticated have centred on the idea of hunter-gatherers bringing wild lambs back to their camps, as pets for their children or to fatten up for later. You can imagine the scenario: a wild ewe has been killed in a hunt, leaving behind a tiny lamb. Hunter-gatherer decides to pick up the lamb and bring it back to the camp. There, it can be looked after by the family and either kept for milk or eaten at a later date.

It makes sense, on the face of it, but there's an issue with weaning – any lamb that was old enough to survive by grazing, rather than its mother's milk, was probably nearly full-size, and not the easiest candidate for a grab and run. Life would be immeasurably easier if you could get a very young lamb and imprint it on a human. That way, it would form such a close attachment to a person that they could control its every move. The only way to do this would be to take a lamb from its mother as soon as it was born and breastfeed it. And so, astonishingly, the history of sheep may indeed start with a woman nursing a newborn lamb.

Far from this being a strange, repugnant idea, anthropology finds modern-day parallels in places such as New Guinea, where young piglets are taken in and nursed alongside children to become part of the family group. Historically, women across cultures have been encouraged to breastfeed young animals for many different reasons (not just for the animal's benefit), including to promote lactation, harden the nipples and prevent conception; indeed, when Mary Wollstonecraft, eighteenth-century writer and feminist philosopher, was dying of sepsis following the birth of her daughter Mary Shelley (who went on to write *Frankenstein*), the post-partum doctor insisted that puppies be brought in to suckle on her breasts and encourage Mary's body to expel the infected placenta. (It didn't work, incidentally, and she died shortly afterwards.)[3] As recently as 2005 the story of a forty-year-old woman, Hla Htay, who was discovered to be breastfeeding a Bengal tiger cub at Yangon Zoological Gardens in Burma, became headline news.[4]

But it's one thing to own a pet lamb and another to start actively keeping and breeding sheep as a source of meat, milk, hides and wool. Neolithic farmers somehow began the journey of turning wild sheep into docile farm animals, ones that would breed in captivity and accept being handled, milked and sheared. We can only guess at the process. As any conservation zoo will tell you, not all animals will breed happily in captivity; from cheetahs to white rhinos, any number of factors – such as stress or mate preference – can stop wild animals from breeding if they're not in their natural habitat. Wild sheep must have coped – or at least enough of them must have done – with the demands of breeding in front of a human audience. Those that didn't, died out.

Sheep had a head start, however, because – down to a quirk of fate – they just happened to be an ideal animal to domesticate. Evolutionary physiologist Jared Diamond came up with a brilliant checklist of six traits that animals must exhibit if they're going to pass the 'domestication test' with flying colours.[5] Lots of animals have some of the traits, but very few have all six. Sheep, however, tick all the boxes.

The first check-box is that the animal can't be too much of a picky eater. They need to be flexible and modest in their eating habits (i.e. to cope with varied grazing or eat more than just one type of foodstuff); the second check-box is that they need to mature quickly so humans don't have to invest years looking after something before it can be eaten or put to some use; the third check-box is, as we already noted, that an animal must be able to cope with being bred in captivity; the fourth is that the creature needs to be docile by nature (although sheep can be aggressive, especially rams during the breeding season); the fifth is that an animal can't be too panicky – deer and gazelle, for example, will often die from shock if captured; and lastly, that a domesticated animal needs to have a social structure that includes a strong leader – this allows groups of animals to be controlled, either by a human taking the position of pack-leader (i.e. a shepherd) or training a dominant animal to lead the flock (i.e. a bellwether sheep).

There's another trait sheep have that made them attractive to early farmers. Some breeds of wild or feral sheep have a distinct sense of place, a strong tendency to stick to their own home range. This natural instinct has been encouraged, over thousands of years, to become a shepherding practice known as 'hefting'. The sheep are so imprinted on a particular area that shepherds can let their flocks graze without fences, hedges or constant rounding up. The sheep get to know where the boundaries of their home range are, where the grass is particularly good, and where to find shelter, and this information is passed from ewe to lamb over successive generations. Hefted flocks also seem to become resistant to particular parasites, toxic plants and mineral deficiencies. Beatrix Potter's favourite sheep, the Herdwick of the Lake District, are perhaps the most famous of all hefted breeds.

Beyond any natural predispositions that made sheep ripe for domestication, we have to assume that early farmers started to select certain characteristics in sheep that made them easier to control – traits such as submissiveness would have been welcomed, while sheep that showed high levels of aggression would have been first for the chop. Sheep that were too large to handle or had horns may have been bred out of the population for being too tricky to manage, and mutations, such as a white fleece (which is easier to dye), selected and bred into the gene pool.

Quite how intentional and rapid this process was, we don't

know – modern sheep vary hugely in size, fleece, colour, whether they have horns and so on – and not all of these characteristics may have been deliberate. However, what we can guess is that wild sheep may have changed into more placid, manageable animals much more quickly than you'd think.

Back in 1959, Soviet scientists began an experiment to see if they could domesticate wild silver foxes, to see what happens to the biology and genetics of an animal as it becomes tame. Every generation the scientists selected and bred from the few foxes that showed friendliness and a lack of aggression.

Fifty years, and fifty generation of foxes, later the experiment showed two remarkable things: one, that it was possible in a relatively short frame of time to take a wild animal and turn it into a domesticated one, not through training but by picking out the tamest offspring; and two, that the tame animals actually *looked* different from their wild ancestors. The genes that were linked with lack of aggression in the foxes also expressed themselves in physical ways – the tame foxes had a cluster of ancillary or accidental traits, such as floppy ears, a shorter nose, white fur spots and a curly tail.[6] In other words, a by-product of domestication was a raft of new physical traits.

It's not impossible that this could have been the mechanism by which some of the characteristics we see in modern sheep came about. DNA analysis has also shown that some of the differences we see between sheep breeds may also be down to responses to climatic changes, as sheep were moved between countries with different terrains and climates. Smaller body size, fleece thickness and other traits may have evolved in response to environmental factors such as humidity or temperature, and not as a result of intensive and intentional breeding.

Whatever the process, we now have a world with around a billion sheep. In this vast, global flock we have at least a thousand breeds and cross-breeds of sheep across the planet, from the huge, fluffy-woolled Merinos to tiny, tough Ouessants. Sheep live on every continent apart from Antarctica, and have adapted to diverse terrains from the freezing mountain ranges of Alaska to the scorching heat of the Sudan desert. Sheep also provide not just meat but milk, cheese, lanolin, sheepskin and, perhaps most importantly, wool.

Sheep have colonized the world so successfully, and show such great variety of breeds, it makes you wonder just how they did it. Piecing together what we can, from both archaeological remains and DNA analysis, it looks as if there were a number of waves of sheep migrations out of the Fertile Crescent. The first wave – the pioneers – may have been domesticated sheep, but they didn't look much different from their wild cousins – they were smaller but still tough, horned creatures with mostly dark, hairy coats. Around seven thousand years ago, these ancient sheep gradually spread across prehistoric Europe, Asia and into North Africa through trade, migration and contact between different cultures.

Descendants of these ovine pioneers still cling on in remote, inaccessible places and have avoided being interbred or replaced by new, 'improved' breeds. If you want to know what a prehistoric sheep looks like, the European Mouflon, which survives in pockets of Sardinia, Corsica and Cyprus, provides a snapshot into the past. As do the sheep which ended up on the windswept, peripheral fringes of Northern Europe – the Soay, the Hebridean, Orkney, Icelandic and Nordic breeds.

These first domesticated sheep weren't particularly useful for their wool. Their coats consisted of thick, coarse hair with only a short undercoat of fine wool – perfect for cool mountain conditions. Every year, these ancient sheep would have moulted. Early farmers may have collected the clumps of hair and wool, or even learned to pluck them from the sheep in a process called 'rooing', but we don't know what they did with the material. The hair would have been brittle, difficult to dye and almost certainly too scratchy to make into clothing, although the softer wool – if you could get any – would have been workable. Meat was the order of the day for these early flocks, and milk soon starts to become a useful secondary product. Scientists recently found what some claim are the remains of the world's oldest cheese – the vestiges of a feta-like sheep's cheese on shards of Croatian pottery dated to 5300 BC.[7]

By 5000 BC, farming had become the main system of food production for a huge swathe of people from West and Central Asia, North Africa and the Mediterranean to Britain, Ireland and Scandinavia. Around this same time, genetic analysis shows that another wave of sheep came out of the Fertile Crescent. These new, 'improved' sheep had been developed with wool in mind and helped shaped the vast majority of modern-day breeds.

This second generation of migrant sheep spread from the Middle East into Europe, Africa and the rest of Asia, breeding, interbreeding and changing as they went. Interestingly, the flow of new, improved sheep didn't just go one way – herders in North China and Mongolia, for example, developed their own unique and successful breeds, which then trotted back to western Asia and into Europe over thousands of years via trade routes, war and conquest. Warriors of Genghis Khan's terrifying Mongol hordes, for example, were said to have ridden west with live sheep strapped to their horses.

It's interesting to note that the wild species of sheep that had entered North America via the land bridge that once linked Russia and Alaska during the last Ice Age were never domesticated by indigenous tribes. America had to wait until the early sixteenth century until it saw a domesticated sheep, when Spanish conquistadors brought over the Churro.

Quite how humans managed to create sheep with thick, soft wool is still a bit of a mystery. Most textile historians would agree that the woolly sheep wasn't 'invented' in a great Eureka moment but would have been arrived at slowly through a series of experiments and accidental mutations.[8] Farmers may have noticed that one particular sheep had an especially fluffy undercoat of wool, or less outer hair than normal, and wondered about the possibilities for fabric and clothing. Once the usefulness of wool was understood, farmers could then speed up the process by selective breeding.

People had been weaving and dyeing materials for thousands of years before wool came along. The earliest evidence for both crafts goes back a staggering 30,000 years, but our prehistoric crafters would have been using plant fibres, such as flax, rather than soft, squishable wool. Imagine, then, how exciting it must have been when people suddenly realized the enormous potential of wool. For archaeologists, however, trying to unravel the history of wool is unenviably difficult – ancient threads so rarely survive down through the centuries. The few scraps that have been found, however, are thrilling because they give us an anchor; a point in time when we can say, with conviction, that wool had arrived.

One of the earliest comes from a dusty site in eastern Iran, near the Afghan border, called Shahr-i-Sokhta. Five thousand years ago, this forbidding, hot territory was a cultural oasis, a city with grand palaces, early writing, pottery and metal craft, and, most significantly, a thriving textile industry. Over the years, archaeologists have uncovered piles upon piles of spindle whorls, used for spinning, as well as well-preserved scraps of woollen textiles, from at least eight different types of fleece.[9]

By the end of the third millennium BC, ancient records uncovered in Iraq, at Ur (one of the world's very first cities), describe at least five categories of wool, with the finest destined, of course, for the royal wardrobe. The texts also describe shepherds controlling vast flocks of sheep - sometimes as many as 27,000 animals in one group - and, for the first time, talk of white sheep.

White wool would have been rare and highly prized, a radical departure from the common brown, piebald and black fleeces that usually made up the flocks. Sheep wool had clearly become a valuable commodity - four times the price of goat hair - and a source of tax revenue for the royal palaces. Laws sprang up to protect sheep farmers and wool merchants from unscrupulous buyers and sheep thieves.[10] Sheep were now worth much more alive than dead.

2

WOOL'S SCALY
SECRET

*A 2,400-year-old woman frozen in time, fireproof
underpants and corsets for Roman soldiers*

In 1993 Natalia Polosmak, a Russian archaeologist, received a tip-off from a local border guard. She and her team were in the formidable Siberian Altai Mountains, a rugged and remote range where Russia, China, Mongolia and Kazakhstan collide. Few archaeologists had ventured to this inhospitable place, but Polosmak had been intrigued by stories she'd heard of ancient horse-riding nomads called the Pazyryk and their burial mounds, which scatter the frozen landscape. The border guard pointed Polosmak to a particular mound – or *kurgan* – marked by a huge pile of boulders and earth. After weeks of digging through layers of rock and soil, the team finally reached a wooden chamber, frozen in ice. Placed outside the chamber were the bodies of six sacrificed horses, harnessed as if ready to ride into the afterlife.

Polosmak and her fellow archaeologists had reason to be excited – since the 1920s, excavations of tombs just like this one had yielded finds that had given the world a tantalizing glimpse into a fabulously rich culture whose people had lived and travelled all over Central Asia more than two thousand years ago. But no one could have anticipated what lay ahead. On opening the wooden chamber, the smell was unmistakable. As one of the researchers later told a PBS documentary:

> You're bailing in buckets constantly. It was damp. You know, when you were inside the tomb your feet were wet. There was a kind of a musty smell to it all, because in fact it had been preserved. So you had the organic materials – wool, wet wool – everyone knows what that smells like. And the horses were strong smelling as well, especially as their stomachs had been preserved.[1]

What Polosmak had uncovered was the elaborate burial of a young, high-status woman, later nicknamed the 'Ice Maiden'. Dead for over 2,400 years, her body and ceremonial offerings had been remarkably well preserved by layers of frozen water. Aged about twenty-five, she was lying on her side, as if fast asleep. The Ice Maiden's head was shaved, with an elaborate wig, and she was spectacularly dressed, wearing a long, wide, crimson and white skirt, woven from sheep's wool and camel hair, cinched at the waist with a tasselled belt, and white woollen thigh-length stockings. But what was most astonishing was her hat: a headdress, three feet (0.9 metres) long, made from felt, which took up a third of the coffin.

What emerged from the discovery, and others in the area, was an understanding of just how important wool was to this ancient group. The Pazyryk were just one of a number of different tribes who have subsequently come to be known under the umbrella name 'Scythians', and shared a similar way of life, language and culture. Siberia is huge, covering one-tenth of the Earth's landmass. Much of it is dense forest or frozen wasteland, but enough land is covered by grassland for nomadic cultures – whose lifestyles centred on herding and hunting – to have emerged around 800 BC.

The Scythians were skilled horse riders, moving herds of sheep and goats from pasture to pasture, following the seasons and travelling vast distances in the process. Adept at endlessly moving camp, they lived in large tents covered with wool felt, floors lined with sheepskin rugs and felt carpets. They were skilled crafters with gold, bronze, wood, horn and leather, but perhaps most astonishing was their mastery of woollen felt; riches uncovered over time have included models of felt swans, felt wall hangings, saddle covers and clothing, including the world's oldest wool trousers. The oldest carpet in the world also came from a fifth-century BC Pazyryk tomb; a freak survivor, the rug had been left behind by early grave robbers who left the mound open to the elements. Water seeped in, soaked the carpet and froze it in time – only for it to be discovered in 1949, its coloured woollen threads as vibrant as the day they were woven.

What's interesting about many of the Scythian wool finds is that they seem to be made from a number of different kinds of fleece, another clue to the exchange and interbreeding of sheep breeds that must have gone on during this period. What's more, many of the dyes and other fabrics that turned up in Scythian tombs come from places far removed from their homeland. Dyes from the Mediterranean, silk from India, woollen textiles from ancient Persia and Armenia – all these cross-cultural influences show just how fluid and wide-spread the exchange of ideas, skills and goods must have been, even 2,500 years ago.

These ancient people took to wool very readily. Sheep's fleece clearly captured their imagination, invited them to craft exquisite items, and weave, knit and felt it into the centre of their culture. And yet, they already had other textiles at their disposal – linen, woven from flax, had been around for centuries by the time wool came along, silk was making an appearance as early as 6500 BC, and both Pakistan and Peru were cultivating cotton only a thousand years later. Wool, by comparison, was a latecomer to the party.

The reason for wool's success is that, even with the advent of modern synthetic materials, there is really no other fibre quite as sublimely adaptable as wool. It's a chameleon; a material that can both repel moisture and absorb it, keep you toasty warm or refreshingly cool depending on the outside temperature, and be soft as silk and yet tough enough to resist searing flames. The secret of sheep's wool rests in its hidden structure; unlike cotton, silk, polyester or linen, wool fibres are cloaked with scales - look at a strand of wool under a microscope and the surface bears an uncanny resemblance to a gnarled tree trunk or a pine cone.

These scales allow wool to do so many miraculous things; like shingles on a roof, these overlapping 'slates' help wool to repel water, and yet water vapour can slip between the small cracks between the scales, where it is absorbed and held inside the core of the fibre. In fact, wool is the most water-loving or 'hydrophilic' of all the natural fibres, capable of absorbing as much as 40 per cent atmospheric water vapour without feeling damp to the touch. This natural tendency to absorb liquids also makes wool easy to dye.

Wool is also a brilliant insulator. Air trapped between the fibres creates a thermal barrier, slowing down the transfer of heat; this means it can keep you cool on a hot day or cosy on a chilly one. But here's the really amazing thing - as wool absorbs moisture, it actually *gives off* heat. So, if you go from a warm, dry house out into a cold, damp evening, your woolly clothes not only absorb the dampness from the air, they actually *generate* warmth. It's a natural chemical process called 'heat of sorption', and also explains why wool, if it's dumped in large heaps or stacked in bales, can become hot all by itself.

Wool is also naturally fire resistant. Thanks to its high nitrogen and water content, wool struggles to burn. And, even if you do manage to set it alight (which is impressive, as wool only lights at around 570-600°C), it tends to smoulder and char, rather than flame. Unlike synthetic fibres, which often combust with alarming ease, wool has an amazing cell structure that swells when it's heated up, forming a natural layer of insulation that resists the spread of any flame. That's why wool blankets are so good at smothering fires and why woollen underwear is a must-have for many firefighters and service personnel.

Perhaps what's so surprising about wool is that, despite our association with soft, cuddly clothes and knitted booties, wool is fantastically robust. Wool fibres can be bent back on themselves over 20,000 times without breaking (to give you a comparison, cotton breaks after 3,000), making them resistant to tearing and abrasion. Wool is also naturally elastic - capable of stretching and then returning to shape - giving it a springiness and resilience that makes it perfect for everything from toddlers' jumpers to piano hammers.

Thinking back to the Scythians, it's interesting that so many finds that came from the Pazyryk burials were felt. When we talk about wool in the Western world, felt isn't the first material that springs to mind - we think of knitted jumpers or worsted suits, perhaps. And yet felt was probably the first fabric made from sheep's wool, and certainly the toughest. To make felt, you don't need any complicated tools or looms - you just need heat, moisture and pressure.

It's all down to the scales on the wool fibres. The process

of rolling, beating and agitating wool fibres together causes these scales to hook on to each other, forming a dense, tear-resistant mat. And, while we don't have any archaeological proof that felt is older than any other type of woollen fabric, it feels safe to assume it probably is; to get wool to a stage where it can be successfully woven takes some effort, as we'll see later. Making felt, on the other hand, is such a simple process it can almost be done by accident; in fact, many of the legends that surround the origins of felt suggest exactly that.

The European version tells the unlikely tale of Saint Clement, a pilgrim who stuffed his shoes with loose wool to protect his feet, only to discover that the constant pressure and sweat transformed the wool into felt. A biblical version tells of the floor of Noah's Ark being transformed into felt carpet by the constant shedding and trampling of animal hairs. In yet another, a Persian shepherd makes felt by accident after stomping on a sheep fleece in frustration.

We'll never know who first made felt from wool, but we can trace its journey from the early nomadic communities of Central Asia, such as the Pazyryks with their 'Ice Maiden', across to the ancient Chinese, Indian and Greek civilizations by the third century BC. Far from being an occasional fabric, felt proved immensely useful – the Pazyryks used it for everything from clothing to headgear, saddle clothes to rugs, while the ancient Chinese made mattresses to sleep on and felt caps for their heads, and the Tibetans crafted large tents, boots and ponchos.[2] But perhaps the most surprising use for ancient felt was body armour.

One of the earliest mentions of Greeks using felt for military uniforms is Homer's description of Odysseus wearing a leather helmet lined with wool. Both Caesar and Thucydides, a Greek historian and general, wrote of soldiers wearing felt vests to deflect arrows, while large felt sheets were hurriedly thrown over military engines and wooden towers if they came under siege.

Roman shields (*scutum*) were often covered with felt, which was then stitched through the wood. Foot soldiers wore 'soft' armour, a quilted felt tunic made of several strips of felt stitched together, either on its own or underneath metal armour, and felt under their helmets to cushion the weight of the metal and absorb the impact of multiple blows to the head. In fact, so much felt was needed to service the ever-growing Roman army that special factories were set up to meet the demand. Records of felt factories come from places such as Brixia (modern Brescia in northern Italy) and Pompeii, which produced a tough, oilskin-like felt strong enough to be used to make everything for fighting men from hats to rigid body corsets. Pliny, writing in the first century AD, notes: '... wool is compressed also for making felt, which when soaked in vinegar is capable of even resisting iron; and what is still more, after having gone through the last process, wool will even resist fire'.

But felt wasn't just for the army. Both the ancient Greeks and

Romans loved the fashion potential and practicality offered by such a hard-working fabric. The Greeks made rain cloaks from it, and a conical fez-like hat called a *pilidion*. These brimless caps were often worn by artisans, travellers and seafarers, but by Roman times, the hat had mutated into something smaller, more like a skullcap, and had come to hold huge symbolic significance. The Roman *pileus* became a potent symbol of liberty: when a slave won his freedom he was allowed to dress as a free citizen, with his toga and felt hat; the Latin phrase *ad pileum vocare* (which literally translates to 'name or call to the cap') came to mean 'to set a person free';[3] Suetonius spoke of a crowd, elated at the death of Nero in AD 68, as the freed, 'felted mob' (*plebs pileata*); and the figure of Liberty, on Roman coins, holds a felt cap in her right hand.

The Romans also had a flattened version of the woollen felt *pileus*, an ancient precursor to the modern beret. The beret has become one of the most eloquent and flexible fashion statements in history; few other pieces of clothing have appealed to both free-thinkers and the military, simultaneously becoming the headgear of choice for the creative intellectual, revolutionary fighter and macho commando.

One of the earliest pictures of anyone wearing a wool beret comes from the Minoan culture of ancient Crete. Clay stamps dating back to 1750-1490 BC show men sporting berets in a ritual procession,[4] but for much of its life, the beret was a working man's cap. It became a hat closely linked with Basque peasants in the foothills of the Pyrenees; headgear perfectly suited to a life of shepherding and changeable weather. By the Middle Ages, berets were a common sight across France, Spain and Italy. Rembrandt, Dutch master of the self-portrait, painted and drew himself many times during the seventeenth century wearing a beret, a tradition later carried forward by artists such as Cézanne, Monet and Picasso.

Artists and intellectuals loved the honest, rural appeal of the humble shepherds' hat, but the woollen beret also caught the attention of the military. The Scots had been sporting 'blue bonnets' since the sixteenth century - soft woollen hats that were knitted, boiled and shrunk-to-fit to create a type of felt - but it was the *Chasseurs Alpins* who first wore the French-style beret we recognize today. Formed in the late 1880s, the *Alpins* are France's elite mountain infantry; the beret proved the perfect combat cap - it was warm, water-resistant and, not having a brim, didn't interfere with a gunman's aim.

The British army soon followed - the Royal Tank Corps were the first to wear the beret as a piece of British service uniform. In 1922, the Colonel Commandant, Lieutenant General Sir Hugh Elles, suggested a black beret to his men after he'd seen the *Alpins* training a few years before. It was the ultimate headgear for the claustrophobically close quarters of a tank - no other hat was as snug-fitting, cheap, could be worn with headphones, or was less likely to get knocked off in the process of climbing in and out of the tank hatch.

The beret soon became seen as the hat of the 'elite force', with the SAS, Parachute Regiment, commandos and many other units soon joining rank. As a symbol of power and military might, the beret was unsurpassed. It was only a matter of time before it drew the attention of revolutionaries and radicals, most famously Che Guevara, Fidel Castro and the Black Panthers in the United States. Felt had come to the front line.

But perhaps the most expansive and consistent use of woollen felt has not been for clothing, but housing. The yurt is now a symbol of glamping, camping's pampered cousin, but its true origins lie in the steppes of Central Asia over 2,500 years ago. In the early 1980s, a bulldozer that was working on a construction site in southwestern Iran accidentally smashed through the wall of a stone funeral chamber. Later called the 'Arjan Tomb', the burial contained all the items one might imagine an ancient king would want for the afterlife - gold bracelets, rings, a dagger, a candelabra, a bronze drinking cup and a large, exquisitely decorated bronze bowl.

One of the most interesting things about the bowl, apart from its breathtaking craftmanship, was that it also displayed the earliest picture we have of a woollen yurt, dating from sometime around 600 BC. Two hundred years later, the Greek historian Herodotus mentions felt dwellings in his descriptions of the Scythian nomads. Alongside terrifying accounts of blinded slaves, warmongering and cannibalistic tribes, he also makes frequent mentions of yurt-like buildings.

In one unusually light-hearted account, he stumbles upon Scythians enjoying a little recreational marijuana: 'The Scythians, as I said, take some of this hemp seed, and, creeping under the felt coverings, throw it upon the red-hot stones; immediately it smokes, and gives out such a vapour as no Grecian vapour-bath can exceed; the Scyths, delighted, shout for joy'.[5]

During the thirteenth century, Genghis Khan commanded his entire empire from a vast woollen yurt. Marco Polo, writing at the time, noted:

the houses of the Mongols are circular and are made of wands covered with felts. These are carried along with them whithersoever they go; for the wands are so strongly bound together, and likewise so well combined, that the frame can be made very light. They also have wagons covered with black felt so efficaciously that no rain can get in. These are drawn by oxen and camels, and the women and children travel in them.[6]

The Mongol Empire rapidly conquered great swathes of the Middle East, Asia and even parts of Europe, helped in no small part by the mobility of their homes – the yurt and the horse gave the Mongols speed and mobility, two of the axioms of successful warfare. Today, 1 in every 200 men alive is thought to be related to Genghis Khan. A team of geneticists recently made the incredible discovery that more than 16 million males in Central Asia have the same male Y chromosome as the great man himself.[7] It seems sheep helped the Mongol Empire subjugate, then populate, the world.

The yurt was, and is, the perfect building for nomadic communities. Collapsible, transportable, and ideally suited to the strong winds that lash the steppes of Central Asia, the yurt supports the life of the sheep-herding family unit and their constant need to move between seasonal grazing areas. The skills to make the felt for the yurts are also alive and well and have changed little over the centuries. The sheep are sheared in both spring and autumn. The fleece is then beaten with sticks to separate the fibres. This fluffed wool is spread out in layers onto a large mat, called the 'mother felt', and sprinkled with water to make it damp. The wet fleece and the 'mother felt' are then rolled up tightly around a long, heavy wooden pole – like a huge Swiss roll – and then wrapped in another layer, usually of yak skin or tarpaulin. This entire man-sized bundle is then dragged behind a horse, like a lawn roller, bouncing and flattening the wool as it goes, until after a few hours the fibres have magically matted together.

Back in 2010, a slow and deadly *dzud*, or 'white death', killed off a staggering 10 million animals in Mongolia, mostly sheep, thanks to an unrelenting summer drought followed by a harsh winter. Many nomadic sheep herders abandoned the steppe to seek their fortunes in Mongolia's capital, Ulaanbaatar, bringing their yurts with them. A yurt ghetto formed, a sprawling shanty-like settlement on the edge of the city.

While many Mongolian herders are shifting away from the traditional ways of living, drawn to cities by the promise of a new, stable life - or forced from their land by the effects of climate change - most still prefer life under a woollen roof. Despite the pressure on them to swap their yurt houses for high-rises, the practical and nostalgic pull of the woollen tent is too strong for a nation that grew on the backs of sheep.

3

WHY SOME SHEEP
ARE SO ROOED

A mummy's tattoos, the invention of scissors
and a ram on the run

Nature has a way of throwing a spanner in the works. Early farmers had – through accident and experiment – finally managed to produce sheep that had softer, woollier fleeces than their wild cousins. These fleeces were ideal for textiles, and yet there was one key problem. Wild sheep had for thousands of years cast off their coats come the warm weather; the wool of these newly domesticated sheep, however, didn't always fall off by itself. By some twist of fate, or perhaps by design, ancient farmers had bred an animal that couldn't undress itself.

In one sense, this was a good thing. If you wanted the wool to be a valuable crop, you needed to be able to predict where it would come off – wild sheep moult anywhere and everywhere, leaving great handfuls to blow away in the breeze. The task became, therefore, how to separate a domesticated sheep from its fleece, especially one that doesn't easily come off.

We have sheep to thank for the invention of scissors. Very early sheep farmers tried many different methods of removing wool, some more painful for the sheep than others. Plucking (also called *rooing*), tearing and combing out wool are mentioned in Mesopotamian texts from the late third millennium BC[1] (cashmere is still harvested by combing in China), while modern comparisons from traditional shepherding communities suggest that some farmers may have cut the wool off using knives – shepherds in Nepal still use a curved, sickle-like knife called an *anise*.

Some archaeologists have suggested that *really* early sheep farmers (i.e. before about five thousand years ago) may have even used stone scrapers to shear their sheep. These expertly knapped, slender stone tools (called tabular scrapers) turn up in the same places that sheep farming first originated – i.e. the Fertile Crescent – and it was originally thought that they were used for scraping animal hides. Two archaeologists had the brilliant idea of finding out if they could use a stone scraper to shear some sheep and then studying the wear-marks on the tool. Remarkably, not only did they discover that the scraper made an admirable job of shearing, but also that the wear patterns were consistent with the ancient scrapers that keep turning up on archaeological digs.[2]

To do a really skilled but swift job of shearing, however, metal shears were unbeatable. Their use is first recorded in a Neo-Babylonian text of about 500 BC.[3] They reach Rome by about 300 BC, and the examples that pop up across Iron Age Europe look remarkably unchanged from the types of shears you might find in an ironmonger's shop today. They're elegant in their simplicity – thin, sharp blades connected by a curve or bow of metal; the bow has a natural spring to it, opening when the shepherd relaxes his or her hand to clip another clump of wool. What's slightly confusing for archaeologists is why shears were needed when many of the breeds that early farmers kept still dropped their wool every year. Why did Iron Age tribes need sheep shears if the wool was going to fall off by itself?

The answer seems to be that, when it comes to ancient breeds – those ancestors of the first migration out of the Fertile Crescent, such as Shetlands and Soays – some have more of a tendency to shed their fleece than others. At one end of the spectrum, there are sheep who drop their fleece so readily that the wool is often blown away before the shepherd can get his hands on it. Some sheep will partially shed their wool, leaving scraggy patches that need to be sheared off. And, at the other end of the spectrum, there are those sheep who never naturally drop their wool and have to be hand-sheared. In other words, for centuries shears and shearing would have been an additional tool in the sheep farmer's kit, but not necessarily always needed. Shears were handy if a farmer got to a patch of fleece that was hard to roo, or for an animal that had lost its ability to moult naturally. In time, however, most sheep lost their ability to shed their wool.

One of the most remarkable pairs of shears ever discovered

came from an Egyptian tomb of the second century AD, in the contents of a woman's work basket. Among her needles, pins and other tools were a pair of exquisite bronze shears - far too lovely for clipping sheep - but they show off the sublime craftsmanship of ancient metalworkers, with their beautiful inlay and decoration. Now sitting in the Metropolitan Museum of Art, these shears are rich with lost meaning - a cat, dog and lion, a god and goddess with plumed crowns, and two falcon-headed sphinxes, all face each other so that when the blades meet, the characters symbolically touch.[4] While we don't know for whom, or why, these shears were made, it's clear they were expensive. The iconography and value of the shears also suggests a ritual function, impossible to know - but what's interesting is just how much superstition and mythology came to surround shears, and shearing, over the following centuries.

In Greek legend, the Fates were portrayed as three women, wool spinners, each assigned a special task. Clotho spun the 'Thread of Life', Lachesis measured out the thread's length, and Atropos snipped off the thread with her shears. The cutting of the thread meant death; a powerful metaphor that came to be synonymous with shears, and their later version, scissors. Shears, in ancient minds, were both invaluable and dangerous, and such objects, with dual meanings, were often ripe for superstitious belief.

Even today, it's considered unlucky to give a pair of shears or scissors as a gift. From Japan to Great Britain, a gift of shears or scissors symbolizes, for many, that the friendship is about to be severed; to avoid the curse, the receiver must 'pay' for the cutting tools with a small token or coin. During New Year festivals, the Chinese avoid using shears or scissors for a month, to prevent a year of quarrelling. In both Egypt and Pakistan, closing and opening shears or scissors without cutting anything, or leaving them open, is also thought to bring bad luck. Shears could also be lucky in certain circumstances; many have been recovered from Iron Age wells, or river beds, where they are thought to have been thrown in for good luck and to appease the gods. During medieval times, shears were often tucked into a new baby's cradle, under a door threshold or placed behind a wall to ward off evil spirits.

Perhaps the best known of all the wool myths, however, is the ancient Greek tale of Jason and the Golden Fleece. Told and retold for over three thousand years, it's the ultimate hero's quest, a 'mission impossible' of challenges, tasks and arduous sea voyages in search of a mythical prize. The task is set for Jason by his evil uncle, King Pelias; if Jason wants to be king, and claim back his rightful throne, declares Pelias, he must first find an oak grove where he will see a golden fleece guarded by a fierce dragon. If he finds the fleece, he must bring it back and his crown will be restored.

Along the way, Jason and his ship's crew, the Argonauts, face murderous wives, winged Harpies, fire-breathing bulls and vicious storms. It's an ancient page-turner, but people have long argued over the significance of the golden fleece – questioning why, in a world of unparalleled treasures, humble sheep's wool should be the ultimate prize.

Two ideas have emerged over the years. Some geologists make the connection between Jason's journey and the history of gold extraction.[5] The mythic quest may have taken its inspiration from a genuine voyage that took place between 3,300 and 3,500 years ago, when an intrepid group travelled from mainland Greece to a find Colchis, a kingdom near the Black Sea which was famed for using sheep fleeces to sift gold dust suspended in mountain streams. The clear creeks of Svaneti, in Georgia, still flow with gold flecks; villagers to this day continue to plunge wool fleeces in the water, the grease of the wool capturing any floating gold particles. After drying, the fleeces are shaken to release the sparking, pure gold dust. Perhaps these glittering fleeces, and the secrets of gold extraction, inspired the myth of the Golden Fleece.

Another theory is that Jason's voyage may reflect just how valuable sheep's wool was to the Greeks and their neighbours. Even as early as 37 BC, the Roman writer Varro identified that flocks of sheep 'on account of their value were said to have golden fleeces, like that of Atreus in Argos [...] or that ram which Aetes sacrificed at Colchis, whose fleece was the quest of those princes known as the Argonauts'.[6] Many early empires not only valued sheep, but worshipped them as founders of wealth, order and civilization. The ram-headed Egyptian god Khnum was thought to have created all the other Egyptian gods and goddesses; Sirtur the Ewe is the goddess of flocks in Sumerian, Babylonian and Akkadian mythology; and Amun, the great Egyptian god of the sun and air, is depicted as a ram-headed sphinx.

The ancient Egyptians even mummified sheep, as a tangible and lasting act of faith; if you felt the urge, you could mummify a favourite animal and present it as a gift to your local temple, or, if you didn't have a dead creature to hand, you could always ask to have an animal mummified and dedicated in your name, which the priest would then bury in the temple cemetery.

Some Egyptians were so taken with sheep that they even had themselves tattooed in their honour. The oldest tattoos in the entire history of civilization were almost missed by accident; hidden on a 5,000-year old Egyptian mummy which had been on display at the British Museum for a century, the dark smudges on the man's arm had been dismissed as being nothing of interest. Recent infrared examination of the marks showed the two marks were actually two tattoos – one of a giant wild bull and the other of a ram. The mummy's choice of tattoos is deeply important – both animals were tough, strong creatures, symbols of the power of brute force. The fact that the mummy turned out to be a young man, aged between eighteen and twenty-one, who had died from a stab wound to his back, certainly paints a picture of a life surrounded by violence and the value placed on physical strength.

Returning to Jason and the Golden Fleece, it's clear that wool was at the heart of Greek culture. As Mary Lois Kissell, pioneering textiles scholar, curator and intrepid fieldworker, described with great enthusiasm in an 1918 *Bulletin* of the Metropolitan Museum of Art,

> Ancient Greek yarns found their way into a great variety of fabrics: into the coarse, every-day apparel for the common people; into the fine, richly flowered, sprigged, and bordered robes for elegant ladies; and into superb funeral robes for the honored dead. No lady of rank allowed the departure of a relative, or hero, without weaving, as a tribute to valor, a sumptuous robe for the burial.[7]

In fact, a great deal of Greek clothing was made from wool; both men and woman wore tunics made from rectangular lengths of wool, fastened together with pins and belts. In cooler weather, a woollen cloak called a *himation* might be thrown around the shoulders, but the overall style of Greek clothing was loose and generous with cloth, all of which required plenty of local wool. Mary Lois Kissell goes on, painting a picture of Greek shepherding that sounds nothing less than idyllic:

The wool for spinning was furnished by great herds of sheep which frequented the mountain slopes of the region. No feature in country life is more delightfully sketched in classic literature than pastoral life and its rustic simplicity. Homer calls Arcadia 'the mother of flocks.' Here imagination peopled the glens and grottoes with dancing nymphs, while shepherd life assumed a fantastic form with Pan chosen 'God of the fleece, whom grateful shepherds love.' A superior quality of wool was obtained, Demosthenes tells us, by giving the 'finest flocks special attention, even to an outer covering of skins to improve the fleece.'

The practice of covering the fleeces of wool sheep still goes on. Wool from Merino sheep is finer than fleece from any other breed - one fully-grown animal can produce enough wool to make three smart business suits. When Merino wool farmers sell their fleeces at auction, the condition of the wool is key - any contamination from mud, poo, pests and vegetable matter can all affect the price, as will problems such as matted or felted fleeces. Sheepcovers - effectively a nylon, ovine Pac-a-Mac - are still used by farmers in the wool industry to keep sheep's coats in pristine condition and increase the value of their produce.

It was also a Merino sheep that demonstrated to the world, only a few years ago, what happens if you fail to shear a modern, domesticated sheep. 'Shrek' was one of thousands of sheep at Bendigo Station, New Zealand, a country where sheep outnumber the human population of 4.3 million by ten to one. Shrek somehow got separated from his flock, and spent the next six years living, gleefully undetected, in nearby caves. When he finally resurfaced in 2004, Shrek was relieved of six times the normal amount of fleece for a Merino sheep – a whopping, record-breaking 60 pounds (27 kg) of wool.

Shrek's plucky survival and record-breaking fleece made him an instant celebrity, and he made numerous public appearances, met the prime minister and even starred in a number of children's books. Incredibly, Shrek's story wasn't the end of it. In 2015 an Australian Merino sheep, 'Chris', who had also been living wild, was finally caught. After being sheared under sedation by national shearing champion Ian Elkins, Chris's fleece was recorded as a staggering 88 pounds (40 kg). Experts believe that both of these sheep, had they been left much longer in the wild unshorn, would have soon expired from carrying so much excess weight in wool.

Australia and New Zealand, of course, take their shearing *very* seriously indeed. In 1788, when Captain Arthur Phillip arrived in New South Wales from Britain, along with his shipful of convicts and livestock, he brought just 100 sheep with the hope of setting up a self-sufficient colony. A century later, the number of sheep in Australia had rocketed to 100 million. Australia proved ideal for wool sheep, with its warm, inland climate and vast areas of natural grassland – but hand shearing could barely keep pace with demand for fleeces. Something was needed to release sheep farmers from the agony and sheer manual grind of hand clippers.

Frederick York Wolseley was an Irish-born wool grower living in Australia; in 1868 he began developing an idea for a shearing machine, the very same year that James Higham, a Melbourne man, patented 'a new apparatus for shearing and clipping wool for sheep and other animals'.[8] Higham's device, which was steam powered, never got off the ground but proved a spur for Wolseley to take his machine to manufacture.

In 1885 Wolseley, with his foreman Herbert Austin, began making his 'shearing machine'. Hand shearers were initially anxious about his new invention, fearful it would soon put them out of work, but Wolseley's demonstrations proved too convincing to ignore. His shears were not only faster and easier to use, they cut off more wool, and at a uniform length, making each fleece much more valuable. The sheep also seemed less stressed and to suffer from fewer cuts and injuries.[9]

Three years later Wolseley returned to Birmingham, England, to set up the Wolseley Sheep Shearing Company. Austin soon followed. Sales of sheep shears proved highly seasonal so, during quiet periods, Austin became interested in building bicycles and dabbling in early motorcars. The Austin Motor Company was founded in 1905 and went on to become one of the largest car manufacturers in the country.

Today, sheep shearing is a competitive business. Despite the introduction of the machine shears, shearing is still a sweaty, physically punishing job. It's also piecework, with earnings relying on speed and skill; while hand-shearers would be lucky to clip more than twenty or thirty sheep in a day, machine shearers can cut ten times that amount. The world record for the most Merino ewes shorn in eight hours currently stands at 497 sheep. Each ewe must carry a fleece with an average weight of 3.4 kilograms and be shorn in eighteen strokes of the shears or less.

And while Merino sheep are valued for their high-quality fleeces, most sheep farmers today find that wool is no longer economically viable to produce – the cost of shearing a sheep is often higher than the value of the fleece. A handful of farmers are rediscovering the benefits of sheep who naturally lose their coats every year, just like their ancient wild ancestors. A new breed – called *Exlana* (which means 'used to have wool' in Latin) – is being developed by farmers in southwest England, who are seeing the benefits of an animal that naturally sheds its fleece in the spring. The coat of the *Exlana* is shorter, hairier and lighter than a traditional sheep, yielding just 1 pound (450 g) of rough, moulted wool. The sheep were developed from exotic and rare breeds, such as the Barbados Blackbelly and the Virgin Islands' native St Croix, which naturally shed their fleeces every year. It's an interesting twist in the history of sheep – one that brings the story of shearing full circle.

4

TOUGH AS OLD
BOOTS

Lactose intolerance, Cyclops the cheesemaker
and a sheep with two heads

Around two thousand years ago, a small band of plucky Celts sailed to the islands of St Kilda, a hundred miles from the coast of mainland Scotland. They brought with them a flock of sheep, ancestors of the modern-day Soays who still live on the island. These small, wiry creatures, who look more like goats than sheep, give us a rare opportunity to imagine what sheep might have looked like in Iron Age Europe, a time-travelling peek at the animals who would have lived with one of the most famed and feared peoples of the ancient world.

The Celts left us no written records of their own to tell us their story, so we must interpret it through the words of the Romans, the glorious artefacts the Celts left behind and the information we can glean from the remains of their homes, settlements and burials. What's emerging is a picture of a world where sheep were central to the survival and aspirations of a rich, independent culture.

The Celts must have eaten plenty of tough, old mutton. From the archaeology, it seems that large numbers of sheep in Iron

Age society were eaten only once their every other function had been exhausted. Although these ancient sheep didn't produce particularly good wool, it seems the Celts kept sheep for their fleeces and milk first, meat second. They were skilled farmers and craftspeople, with a well-organized cloth industry that didn't go unnoticed by the ever-watchful Romans. Strabo, a Greek historian of the time, notes: 'Their wool is rough and thin at the ends, and from it they weave their thick *sagi* [coats] which they call *laenae*.'[1]

In fact, one piece of Celtic woollen clothing really caught the eye of Romans, who needed something to warm the cockles of their advancing soldiers and the expats who made the northern provinces their home. The *birrus Britannicus* was a kind of duffel-coat-cum-hoodie made by the local tribes. A Roman mosaic from Chedworth Villa in Gloucestershire illustrates beautifully how the two cultures often rubbed alongside each other, sharing influences and trade; in it, a man wears a *birrus* while holding a hare, the *birrus* a Celtic influence, the hare a Roman import.

The woollen *birrus* proved a hit and was exported across the Roman Empire in vast numbers. The trade was clearly so brisk that in AD 301 Emperor Diocletian felt the need to levy huge taxes on the *birrus* and the *tapete Britannicum*, a multi-purpose Celtic rug. Prices for a fine *birrus* were steep at 6,000 denarii, roughly the equivalent of 500 litres of wine or a quarter of a year's salary for a teacher.[2]

The Romans also liked other 'barbarian' fashion choices – Emperor Augustus, who struggled with cold weather and had a weak constitution, took to wearing clothes and materials 'borrowed' from conquered tribes across Northern Europe, including woollen vests and trousers. In the first century AD, Pliny writes of his fellow Romans clamouring for the latest item from the provinces – the shaggy *bardocucullus*, a windproof cloak waterproofed by the lanolin left in the wool.

What's interesting is just how many sheep the Celts would have needed to keep, not only if they were making and exporting cloaks, but also for their own domestic use. Iron Age Soay-like sheep shed only about 2.2 pounds (1 kg) of wool every year – that would mean a family of two adults and three children would have needed about twenty sheep just to keep themselves in coarse woollen blankets and garments.[3] But, it seems, the Celts had no problems with large-scale farming, raising impressive numbers of sheep and trading on an international basis. Strabo, whom we met earlier, agrees: 'They have such enormous flocks of sheep and herds of swine that they afford a plenteous supply of sagi [woollen coats] and salt meat, not only to Rome but most parts of Italy.'[4]

The hardy, diminutive sheep were good at adapting to the varied terrain Britain had to offer, from the rugged Welsh highlands to the undulating chalk plains of Wessex, but the creatures were also useful beyond their potential for meat and wool. Ancient sheep would have been a valuable source of dung, not only as a fertilizer for fields and crops but also to provide fuel. Many pastoral communities still use dried dung (or dung cakes) as a ready, free supply of heat energy – from cow and camel dung in modern Egypt to goat and sheep dung in Mongolia.

Sheep's milk would have also been drunk by the Celts; the celebration *Imbolc*, on 1 February, was one of the four major ancient Celtic festivals – a day to give thanks for the gift of spring lambs and ewes' milk. It's an interesting quirk of human evolution that some cultures can tolerate milk, while others can't. Before the domestication of animals such as sheep and cows, only babies could digest a sugar found in milk, called lactose. Babies do this by making an enzyme called lactase. For most of human history, however, the ability to digest lactose stopped after weaning.

Ancient cultures who wanted to use sheep's milk had to first ferment it, which got rid of lactose but also, crucially, destroyed some of its caloric value. Anyone who could digest animal milk without first needing to ferment it could therefore gain an additional energy advantage. In other words, those ancient cultures that relied on dairy foods, including sheep's milk, as a vital source of nutrition, created a survival pressure on the members of their group. Those lucky few people who could absorb lactose were more likely to survive and pass on their genes, including those for lactose digestion.

Recent analysis of the DNA of ancient skeletons from

Europe and Russia suggests that the mutation required for lactose tolerance appeared about 4,500 years ago and spread throughout the European population. This ability to digest milk would have been particularly beneficial for groups who had migrated to cooler, temperate places in Europe as it was an additional way of getting Vitamin D, the other main source being sunlight which, in those regions, can be in short supply (hence only 2 per cent of people in Denmark are lactose intolerant, compared to virtually 100 per cent of Zambians).[5] Estimates suggest between a third and half the population of the world cannot digest lactose or suffer from lactose intolerance. It's particularly common among African, East Asian, Southeast Asian and Native American populations.

While Iron Age tribes from all over Europe were probably able to digest and enjoy sheep's milk straight from the pail, that doesn't mean they didn't make other things from it. Sheep's milk butter, yoghurt and cheese were almost certainly part of the Celtic diet; Pliny, in his *Natural History*, lovingly devotes an entire chapter to 'Various Kinds of Cheese' and mentions many from the 'provinces', including the cheese of Ceba, 'which is made from the milk of sheep', and a pungent goats' cheese from Gaul. Some Roman writers considered sheep and goat milk to be far superior to cow's milk,[6] and the most nourishing, and it's interesting that modern science bears this out. Sheep's milk has a far higher fat and protein content than goat or cow's milk, and greater levels of calcium, magnesium, zinc and other minerals.[7]

Making cheese from sheep's milk wouldn't have been a novelty among the Iron Age tribes and the cheese-loving Romans. As we saw in Chapter One, feta-like varieties have been knocking around for at least seven thousand years and were probably the result, at first, of a happy accident. Early farmers and herders had to be resourceful when it came to carrying supplies of water and milk. The inflated stomachs and bladders of dead sheep proved to be excellent carriers for liquids. The stomachs of ruminant animals also contain an enzyme, however, called rennet, which causes milk to coagulate and separate into curds and whey. Perhaps, goes the theory, some of the residual rennet in these sheep-stomach carriers caused the milk in them to curdle and create cheese.

However it started, sheep's cheese soon proved an invaluable and popular foodstuff – not only was it nutritious, but it also kept much longer than raw milk. In hotter climates, such as the Middle East, salt was often added to cheese to keep it from spoiling – *jameed*, a Bedouin cheese, for instance, was traditionally made in late spring from sheep or goat's milk, heavily salted, shaped into balls and dried out in the sun. Preserved in this way, *jameed* could keep for months, all its nutrition and goodness locked away until needed.

In cooler, Northern European countries, this type of preservation didn't suit the damp, temperate climate. Instead, communities found different ways of preserving their sheep's milk, such as smoking cheeses or allowing moulds such as *penicillium roqueforti* and *penicillium glaucum* to grow, which don't just impart flavour but also have antibacterial properties.

A cheese sounding suspiciously similar to Roquefort gets a mention in Pliny's hit list of favourite cheeses as early as the first century AD ('made in Gaul [and] has a strong taste, like that of medicine').[8] According to legend, the world's most famous blue cheese was first discovered when a shepherd was eating his lunch of sheep's curd cheese and bread in a cave. As he was eating, he spotted a beautiful young woman outside and, deciding to pursue her, left his lunch behind. After days of fruitless searching, the lovestruck shepherd returned to the cave only to find the cheese and bread had both developed mould. Starving, he ate the cheese, only to discover that the mould had transformed it into sublime, tangy Roquefort. Today, sheep's milk Roquefort is still made in the caves of Mont Combalou in south-central France.

Sheep's cheese also makes a starring appearance in the Greek myth of Odysseus and the Cyclops. It's a well-known tale, one we think we know, about a one-eyed giant blinded by the Greek hero, but Homer's *Odyssey*, which was written almost three thousand years ago, also gives food historians a wonderfully detailed account of early cheesemaking. And while tales of derring-do and battle-hardened men grab the attention of schoolchildren, ancient descriptions of shepherding and 'Cyclops the artisan cheesemaker' are just as thrilling for those of us switched on by the history of food and farming:

We soon reached [the Cyclops] cave, but he was out shepherding, so we went inside and took stock of all that we could see. His cheese-racks were loaded with cheeses, and he had more lambs and kids than his pens could hold. They were kept in separate flocks; first there were the hoggets, then the oldest of the younger lambs and lastly the very young ones all kept apart from one another; as for his dairy, all the vessels, bowls, and milk pails into which he milked, were swimming with whey [...] he drove all the ewes inside, as well as the she-goats that he was going to milk, leaving the males, both rams and he-goats, outside in the yards [...] When he had so done he sat down and milked his ewes and goats, all in due course, and then let each of them have her own young. He curdled half the milk and set it aside in wicker strainers, but the other half he poured into bowls that he might drink it for his supper.[9]

While *The Odyssey* paints a colourful picture of sheep-keeping in eighth-century BC Greece, and remains one of the oldest surviving great works of Western literature, the Iron Age tribes who lived only a few hundred years later remain silent in terms of the written word. And so it's up to archaeologists to try to read the motives, fears and preoccupations of these extraordinary people, from the things they left behind. One of the most challenging bits of Iron Age behaviour to try to understand is why they seemed to sacrifice so many living things, including people and sheep. And, while the ritual killing of creatures and humans was certainly nothing new by the time the Celts came along, it seems it was both endemic and central to their everyday life.

We already know that sheep were an integral part of Celtic daily life and its economy. It's thought that these domesticated creatures, who played such a significant role in day-to-day living, were also some of the most likely to play a role in sacrificial rituals (along with other farmyard favourites, horses, dogs and pigs). Sacrifice had to *cost* something to the people who were doing it, otherwise the gesture held no value. If you were going to ask for a favour from the fickle gods, or for protection from malevolent forces, you needed to 'pay' for those requests with something that represented a deliberate loss to your own pocket or community. Sacrificing a sheep, therefore, not only meant the loss of an animal, but also all the potential wool, milk, manure, cheese, and future lambs that creature would have given you.

What's fascinating is just how varied sheep sacrifices were in Iron Age Britain and further afield - it seems there were few occasions that didn't warrant a gruesome ritual. Sheep could be sacrificed as a gesture of thanks, for a good harvest for example, or for recovery from a disease. Sacrifices were needed for fertility rituals, often with young or pregnant sheep. They could be used for divination - parts of the animal would be used to foretell the future (in Rome, a *haruspex*, or 'gut gazer', was the official job title of someone who could predict the future based on the entrails and offal of sacrificed sheep), or to communicate with the gods.

Sheep were thrown into empty grain-pits or wells as a gift of thanks, and consumed in vast ritual feasts. Sheep might be buried with their owners, as part of the funeral cortège, or presented as joints of meat as 'food offerings' for the afterlife. Interestingly, unlike daily life – when tough old mutton was the meat of necessity – in sepulchral contexts young lambs were often chosen instead – 'the dead liked their meat tender'.[10]

One of the most fascinating uses of sheep sacrifice was as a 'foundation offering', the placing of an animal under the walls or floors of a building as an offering to the gods. In some instances, the sacrifices were human, not ovine, and there are well-documented examples of whole and parts of bodies deliberately interred under Iron Age structures and ramparts.[11] More often, however, sacrifices were animals, buried in significant places and positions, to bring luck to a new building. Similar offerings were also made when a house or other important building had come to the end of its useful life, called a 'termination offering'.

What's surprising, perhaps, is just how long the tradition continued – well into Europe's early Middle Ages. Two halves of a sheep's jaw bone were found, for example, deliberately placed as a foundation offering, under Trig Lane, London, dating from the 1300s.*

New discoveries bring up interesting questions for archaeologists, often challenging long-held beliefs; one particularly attention-grabbing example came from an Iron Age site near Winterborne Kingston in Dorset. While ancient Greek and Egyptian cultures had long practised the rather gruesome ritual of splicing and burying different animals together to form mythical hybrid beasts, it had never been something that we thought had interested the ancient Britons.

And then, as often happens, the archaeology threw us a curveball; the discovery of bones, on an Iron Age settlement, that had been deliberately rearranged to form fantastical creatures, half one animal and half another. Among the monstrous creations were horse-cow combinations, a dog–cow fusion and a sacrificed push-me-pull-you sheep with two heads – its own and one from a bull. There was a young woman as well, also sacrificed and laid on a bed of animal bones (including sheep), the bones mirroring, in shape, the skeleton of the dead woman. Most of the sacrifices were dated to the first century BC and found under the entranceways to the houses on the site, leading archaeologists to conclude that these were probably decommissioning or termination rituals, giving thanks for those buildings which had outlived their purpose.[12]

---

* The same site also threw up a pair a spectacles. Made in 1435, they're the earliest and most complete glasses ever found in England.

It's easy to consign such seemingly peculiar practices to ancient history, and yet it isn't difficult to find accounts of peculiar sheep rituals from relatively recent times; in her 1910 publication *Sacrificial Customs and other Superstitions in the Isle of Man*, local writer Sophia Morrison collected reminiscences from the island: 'Mr. A. W. Moore [...] gives an account of an *oural losht* (burnt-offering) in the parish of Jurby in 1880, remarking that even within the last five years there have been several sacrifices [...] Such a method would naturally be supposed to have belonged to past ages only, if there was not evidence that lambs have been burnt on May Day eve or May Day [...] within living memory.'

Sophia goes on:

Manx people sometimes put into their purses the lucky bone of the sheep. A young woman accidentally dropped one out of her purse before me yesterday. The bone is shaped like Thor's hammer. I have been told that if a traveller loses his way at cross-roads, not knowing which path to take, he throws the sheep's lucky bone before him, and then follows that path towards which the hammer-end points.[13]

Muslims around the world still value sheep sacrifice as an important annual reassertion of their faith. Eid al-Adha is the 'Festival of Sacrifice', falling on the tenth day of the holy month of Dhu al-Hiijah. An ancient tradition, it is done to honour Abraham's willingness to kill his own son, Ishmael, at Allah's request; thankfully, in the story, Allah intervenes and stops Abraham making the ultimate sacrifice and a sheep takes Ishmael's place. Today, a sheep (or goat, cow or camel depending on local tradition) is sacrificed in memory of the story, not only as a way of remembering Abraham's devotion but also to serve as a reminder not to become too attached to physical possessions at the cost of spiritual wealth. The animal is then divided into three – one third going to the poor, one to friends and relatives, and one to the immediate family.

We also have Iron Age sacrifices – in particular, bog bodies – to thank for some of our knowledge about ancient woollen textiles, their manufacture and trade. They're grisly, fascinating finds – people who were ritually killed and thrown in Northern European wetlands between 800 BC and AD 200 – and yet they continue to yield clues about an ancient way of life. Bog bodies are unusually well preserved – thanks to the acidic, oxygen-poor peat bogs, the skin, hair and woollen clothes of many of these unfortunates remain remarkably intact.

Many of the bog bodies display evidence of particularly nasty ends – slit throats, stoven heads, nooses around necks. This has led many historians and archaeologists to conclude that the victims were probably slaves, criminals or prisoners, an idea bolstered by the Roman historian Tacitus, who wrote in AD 98: 'The punishment varies to suit the crime. Traitors and deserters are hanged on trees; the cowardly, the unwarlike and those who disgrace their bodies are drowned in miry swamps under a cover of wicker.'[14]

And yet not all archaeologists agree. Recent research is offering a different explanation, at least for some of the bog bodies. Rather than being outcasts and criminals, some of the victims of the bog may have been distinguished members of their communities, perhaps even chosen for their prestige. It may have been an honour to be sacrificed and some victims went, perhaps, voluntarily to their watery graves.

Some of the woollen clothing worn by bog bodies reveal fascinating insights into Iron Age lives. The clothes of Huldremose Woman, for example, a Danish bog body discovered in 1879 and almost two thousand years old, show a woman lavishly dressed in a check woollen skirt and scarf, and two sheepskin capes. The National Museum of Denmark describes her clothes in detail:

> The skirt was tied at the waist with a thin leather strap inserted into a woven waistband. The scarf was wrapped around the woman's neck and fastened under her left arm with a pin made from a bird bone. On her upper body she wore a cape made from several dark brown sheep skins, with a collar of light-coloured sheep skin. The wool side of the skin cape was turned outwards. Under this was another cape with the wool side turned inwards. This was made from 11 small dark lamb skins. The cape had been

used a great deal and had 22 patches sewn on [...] The woman's long hair was bound up with a woollen cord, which was also wound round her neck several times. She also wore another wool cord around her neck, on which hung two small amber beads.

Analysis of the wool and sheepskin has thrown a number of spanners in the works, challenging what we thought we knew about Iron Age people. Popular myth has long reinforced the image of ancient tribes dressed in wild furs and drab, plain-coloured clothing. Not so. Most of the skins on Huldremose Woman came from domesticated animals and, what's more, represented a significant cost in terms of the amounts of animals involved. Her two capes would have used the skins of at least fourteen sheep – an unlikely expense for a criminal or a person of low status.

Her clothes were also brightly coloured, using red and purple-blue dyes that would have been expensive. Textile scientists have established that our Iron Age ancestors had access to some glorious colours: yellows from plants such as weld, saw-wort, broom and chamomile, as well as from buckthorn berries; blue from woad; red from lady's bedstraw, dyer's woodruff and madder; purple from lichen; and black from tannin.[15]

Recent chemical analysis on Huldremose Woman revealed yet another surprise – that her woollen clothes were made not locally, but probably miles away in northern Sweden or Norway. Researchers could also tell that she'd travelled extensively before she'd died. Quite why a well-travelled forty-year-old woman, dressed in fine woollen clothes and jewellery, was sacrificed and then carefully laid out with her arms bound, we will never know. One thought is that she may have been the hostage of a raiding party who had invaded her territory; another theory is that she was a person of prestige whose special status entailed a good deal of travel. All we know is that two thousand years ago a small farming community felt compelled to sacrifice an important woman and consign her body and her valuable woollen clothes to the bog. Few onlookers to this act of explosive violence, including the Iron Age sheep, however, would have batted an eyelid.

5

RHYMES AND
RIDICULOUS CURES

Bumfits, black sheep and the wrong star sign

Sheep have changed our language. They've trampled their way into our sayings and superstitions, appearing in place names and poems. We talk about a person being a 'dyed-in-the-wool conservative' or a 'wolf in sheep's clothing', we sing 'Baa, Baa, Black Sheep' to our children and guard against being 'fleeced' by scammers.

When we use these words, however, we rarely think about where they come from. 'Shoddy', for example, now used as an adjective to describe something that is badly made, once referred to a yarn made from recycled wool; woollen rags were shredded into fibres and then mixed with a small amount of new wool to make a cheap material also known as rag wool. To be on 'tenterhooks' (sometimes mistakenly rendered as 'tenderhooks') harks back to the practice of wet woollen cloth being stretched on a wooden frame called a 'tenter', where it was fastened in place with hooks so that it dried nice and taut, without shrinking. Unpicking the threads of these linguistic relics reveals a past where sheep, wool and shepherding were the focus of a community and its way of life.

But let's start with a little known, deliciously quirky remnant called the 'shepherds' score', or *Yan Tan Tethera*. It's an ancient way of counting, still used by some shepherds today, in northern England, Wales, parts of the southwest and lowland Scotland. The system is vigesimal, or base-20. It stops at twenty – once a shepherd had counted to this number, he'd mark it in some way (a notch on his crook, perhaps, or a stick placed in the ground) and then start again at one.

Linguistically, its origins are lost, but some scholars believe it may have its roots in Brittonic (or Brythonic) languages, those early versions of Welsh, Cornish and Breton spoken during the Iron Age. Individual words vary slightly from region to region, but they all share remarkable similarities. The Lincolnshire version goes like this:

Yan (1), Tan (2), Tethera (3), Pethera (4), Pimp (5), Sethera (6), Lethera (7), Hovera (8), Covera (9), Dik (10), Yan-a-dik (11), Tan-a-dik (12), Tethera-dik (13), Pethera-dik (14), Bumfit (15), Yan-a-bumfit (16), Tan-a-bumfit (17), Tethera-bumfit (18), Pethera-bumfit (19), Figgot (20)

The numbers above ten use a combination of smaller digits – so eleven is Yan-a-dik (one and ten) – it's brilliant in its simplicity and rhythmic bounce when spoken aloud, so it's perhaps no surprise that there are records of both knitting songs based on *Yan Tan Tethera* and playground counting games. *Yan* is also still in common use as a Yorkshire dialect word for 'one'. There's lots of fun to be had adding the numbers together – who would have thought, for example, that a *pimp* and a *dik* make a *bumfit*?

Another children's favourite is, of course, 'Baa, Baa, Black Sheep':

> Baa, baa, black sheep,
> Have you any wool?
> Yes, sir, yes, sir,
> Three bags full;
> One for the master,
> And one for the dame,
> And one for the little boy
> Who lives down the lane.

The words of this rhyme have scarcely altered over the years, apart from the last line, and it's this that may give a clue to its original message. In an early version, which appeared in the collection *Mother Goose's Melody* in the mid-eighteenth century, the last line reads 'But none for the little boy who cries in the lane'.* One interpretation has been that the rhyme

---

* BAH, bah, black Sheep,
  Have you any Wool?
  Yes, indeed have I.
  Three Bags full;
  One for my Master,
  One for my Dame,
  But none for the little Boy
  Who cries in the Lane.
  Source: www.bl.uk/collection-items/mother-gooses-melody

is actually much older than we imagine, perhaps even dating as far back as the late thirteenth century.[1]

In the late thirteenth century, King Edward I imposed a swingeing tax on wool. He needed to raise money to fight the French, and the British wool trade, which was a vastly successful industry at the time – as we shall see later – was an easy target. Initially, the government's plan was to simply take all the country's stocks of wool and confiscate them for 'safe custody', so they couldn't be exported to France. Actually, what the government planned to do was to export the wool themselves and keep the profit.

Wool merchants were, of course, furious and rose up to complain bitterly. In response, Edward I scrapped the confiscation plan and decided, instead, to stick extra duty on each bag of wool destined for sale; the tax became known as the *maltolt*, or 'bad tax'. The king justified the tax on the grounds that he was risking his life in war and 'his grateful subjects should happily pay their taxes'.[2] Wool merchants saw things very differently and, angry at having to pay such high taxes on their wool, passed the costs onto the wool farmers, forcing them to accept low prices for their fleeces.

'Baa, Baa, Black Sheep' may, therefore, be a reference to this difficult period, when taxes on wool were so high that only the 'master' (the king) and the 'dame' (the merchants) made any money from the industry, while the weeping little boy represents the shepherds and wool farmers who went home empty-handed.

The reference to the 'black sheep' in the rhyme is trickier to interpret. Black sheep have been both loved and loathed in equal measure over the centuries. In terms of wool production, black sheep among a white flock were problematic. Black wool is difficult to dye, and so a black sheep in a white flock destined for cloth would have represented a financial loss. The coat colour of wild sheep is usually a dark body with a pale tummy, but over the centuries shepherds strongly selected for a uniform, white coat which was easy to dye. The gene for dark fleece didn't disappear, however; it is simply recessive – in other words, a white sheep can carry the black fleece gene within a flock, but you wouldn't be able to tell which animal it was until it produces a black lamb.[3]

The arrival of a black sheep from a white flock must have left ancient shepherds scratching their heads, bewildered by nature's alchemy. And so perhaps it's no surprise that black sheep became the target for superstitions and peculiar folk remedies. An early reference to the healing 'magic' power of black sheep appears in an Old French collection of women's folk beliefs that was translated into English around 1507 as the *Gospelles of Dystaues* (or Distaff Gospels). A cure for smallpox involved wrapping yourself in a black sheepskin: 'Yf a woman haue the small pockes, it behoueth that her husbande bye her a blacke lamb of the same yere, and after bynde her in the skynne, and the let hym make hys pylgrymage and offrygne to saynt Arragonde,* and for a trouthe she shall hele.'[4]

Nearly four hundred years later people were still using a similar 'cure' in the Outer Hebrides: 'When a man was afflicted with pains in his joints, a black sheep, still living, was placed over the rheumatic limbs of the patient.'[5]

Records of folklore show a rather schizophrenic approach to black sheep; at the end of the nineteenth century it's recorded that 'one black sheep is regarded by the Sussex shepherds as an omen or good luck to his flock', while across the water in Ireland, 'If the first lamb born of the season is born black, it foretells mourning garments for the family within the year.' In Kent 'a black lamb foretells good to the flock', whereas in Orkney 'It is unlucky to see a black lamb as the first of the season.'[6]

The idea that black sheep stand out from the rest of the flock, for good or ill, probably explains the phrase 'black sheep of the family', someone who's a disappointment or wayward character within in a group. It's a near universal idea – *la pecora nera* in Italian, *das schwarze Schaf der Familie* in German,

---

* *Saynt Arragonde* was a misspelling of Saint Radegonde, a sixth-century Thuringian princess and Frankish queen who – after leaving her abusive husband Clotaire I – went on to found the Abbey of the Holy Cross at Poitiers, France. The patron saint of several French and English churches, and of Jesus College, Cambridge, she was also included in certain healing prayers, namely for fever, scabies, leprosy, scabs and ulcers. She was also the patron saint of bad marriages.

France's *brebis galeuse* and *mouton noir, svartur sauður* in Icelandic, and so on, with some interesting regional twists; the Croatians say '*Da vidimo čija majka crnu vunu prede*', meaning 'we see whose mother is spinning black wool'. Ironically, the country that has the greatest number of sheep – mainland China – doesn't use the phrase; the Mandarin equivalent is *hài qún zhī mǎ* – 'the horse that brings trouble to the herd'.

Sheep are, however, pivotal to Chinese mythology and celebrations. The Chinese zodiac consists of twelve animals, each one with its own distinct character. Dating back to the fifth century BC, this ancient classification system subscribes to the idea that a person's destiny can be determined by the astrological 'climate' at the time of their birth, including the position of the planets, moon and sun.

Each year is a creature – the animals follow each other in a predictable twelve-year cycle: rat, ox, tiger, rabbit, dragon, snake, horse, sheep, monkey, rooster, dog and pig. Each animal has unique set of traits which people born in those years are said to possess. Over the past hundred years or so, the 'Year of the Sheep' fell on these years – 1907, 1919, 1931, 1943, 1955, 1967, 1979, 1991, 2003, 2015 – and it's a sign said to be dominated by an easy-going, but perhaps frustrating, docility. Those born under the sign of the sheep are, in Chinese culture, thought to be peace-loving, gentle and patient, but also timid, shy about leadership and prone to complain.

The Year of the Sheep is also known, confusingly, as the Year of the Goat and the Year of the Ram. The Chinese word *yang* refers to the subfamily *caprinae*, which includes sheep, goats, ibex and all manner of cloven-hoofed creatures. In Vietnam the equivalent, *Mùi*, is unequivocally a goat, however, while in Japan *Hutsuji* is a sheep. Whatever the interpretation, however, the character traits remain distinctly passive and self-effacing. How different, then, from the Western equivalent – Aries. For followers of astrology, those born under the sign of the ram are said to be headstrong, impulsive and restless; natural born leaders with a will of iron but little sensitivity.

It is interesting that the Western zodiac uses the hot-headed, virile characteristics of a ram rather than the placid temperament of a sheep. The shape of the constellation Aries is often interpreted as that of a male sheep, but it requires a leap of visual imagination that stretches credibility. To find clues to the origins of the star sign, we need to understand how the Western zodiac first came about.

The Babylonians, who lived over three thousand years ago, wanted to make sense of how the Earth, sun and stars moved through the sky. They imagined a straight line drawn from Earth, through the sun, and out into the stars. This line would point at different constellations depending on the time of year. They divided the year into thirteen constellations at first, and then changed it to twelve (as it fitted neatly into their existing twelve-month calendar), each constellation represented by a mythical character.

The sign that was to become Aries wasn't a sheep at first but was known in Babylonian texts as the 'Hired Man'. It is not clear when the man became the ram, but it may have had something to do with sacred healing rituals. Priests in Babylonian times would decide which ingredients to use in a healing ritual based on your astrological sign – the remedy for someone born under the sign of the 'Hired Man' involved being anointed with 'sheep-blood, sheep-fat, and sheep-hair'.[7] Aries was also the constellation that could be seen at the same time as the vernal equinox, the beginning of spring and the time of renewed life and regrowth. The choice of a ram would have been apposite for that time of year – the ram being a potent symbol of fertility, rebirth and strength.

Most of us know our star signs, even if we don't believe in them, but few of us realize that since the zodiac was first devised all those centuries ago, the constellations' positions have actually drifted, owing to an astronomical quirk called *precession* (which has to do with the Earth wobbling on its axis). So your 'real' zodiac sign is actually different from the one you think it is. Aries, for example, are supposedly born between 20 March and 20 April – as this was the month when ancient astrologers could see the constellation of the ram. Now, the sun is no longer within this constellation during those days and instead Aries falls between 18 April and 13 May, a month later than it used to. Thought you were a hooligan, hell-raising ram? You're actually a touchy-feely Pisces.

It's interesting that the different characteristics of ewes and rams have entered into common phrases over time. The words 'ewe' and 'sheep' are interchangeable – depicting a gentle creature, prone to quietness and acquiescence. The ram, in contrast, is always about brute force, impulsivity and virility. The word 'sheepish', for example, probably comes from the thirteenth-century Old English word *sceaplic* – meaning 'like a sheep' – and is written down in its current form as early as the 1690s; we use it to mean bashful or shy about coming forward. Phrases and words such a 'battering ram', 'to ram' or 'rammed' have their roots in the noun 'ram'. Ram is an interesting word with an mysterious etymology – in Proto-Germanic (the language spoken across parts of Northern Europe after 500 BC) *rammaz* could mean both strong and powerful but also smelly. It's not clear whether rams were named for their brute strength or their poor personal hygiene. Interestingly, the Scots still use the word 'ram' to mean a bad whiff.

Some phrases have fallen out of use in recent times: to cast a 'sheep's eye' at something or someone was to give an admiring or longing look; a 'sheep-biter' was a shifty, thieving person – in Shakespeare's *Measure for Measure* the foppish Lucio demands that the duke show his 'sheepe-biting face' – which in turn came from the meaning of a dog that worries or nips at sheep; and a 'mutton-monger' or 'muttoner' was an lascivious insult, used between the sixteenth and nineteenth centuries, to describe a promiscuous man, based on the slang term 'mutton' which meant prostitute (and also, charmingly, vagina). We still use the bitchy phrase 'mutton dressed as lamb' to describe an older woman in a young person's clothes without realizing its original sexual double meaning.

'Don't spoil the sheep for a halfpenny worth of tar' is often misquoted as 'ship' rather than 'sheep' but hasn't affected the meaning of the phrase - i.e. don't allow penny pinching to spoil the finished product. The phrase appears regularly from the early 1600s - examples such as 'A man will not lose a hog [a young sheep] for a half pennyworth of tar'[8] - tar being used as a shepherds' home-made remedy for sores and wounds on sheep. It's a delightful coincidence that the phrase works just as well referring to the tarring of ships to make them waterproof, but sheep were the initial reference point.

In fact, the misquote may have stemmed from the fact that 'ship' was an early word for sheep; there are hundreds of ovine place names in Britain that begin with Ship, Shap, Shep or Skip - most of them throwbacks to the Anglo-Saxon and Viking eras. In Yorkshire, for example, there's Skipton (meaning 'sheep town'), Skipwith (sheep farm) and Shipley (sheep clearing or meadow) to mention just a handful. In Somerset, there's Shepton (sheep farm), Shapwick (sheep village), Shipham (sheep home) and Shiplate (sheep stream).

Lots of others spring to mind - both Shiplake in Oxfordshire and Shipbourne in Kent also mean 'sheep stream'; Shepshed in Leicestershire (sheep headland); and the Island of Sheppey is literally 'sheepy island'.[9] Other sheep-inspired words sneak their way into place names – Wetherby in Yorkshire ('sheep's town' – *wether* is still used by farmers to mean a castrated ram), Woolwich (place for trading wool) and Easter in Essex (from the Old English *eowestre* meaning 'sheepfold').

This last word also makes an appearance in Osterley, meaning 'sheepfold in the clearing or meadow'. Ironically, one of the sheepiest sounding of places, Wool, in Dorset, has nothing to do with sheep, but comes from the Old English *wiell*, a spring. Some sheep names are well hidden, such as High Boughthill in Northumberland (a *bought* is a sheepfold), Billia Croo off the west coast of Orkney (*croo* is a sheep pen), Hog Hill and Hog Rigg in the Scottish borders (a *hog* being a young sheep), Shiels in Aberdeenshire and Shepherdshield in Northumberland (a *shiel* or *shield* is a shepherd's summer hut) and Wedder Law in Dumfries and Galloway (*wedder* is the same as *wether*).[10]

The phrase to achieve something 'by hook or crook' – by whatever means possible – may also be related to sheep. In early medieval England, when the land was cloaked with trees, commoners were allowed certain feudal rights to collect firewood from the forests (we'll find out more about common land later in the book). It's said that people were allowed to cut off branches as far as the 'hook and crook' could reach – the hook being a billhook (a curved knife) and the crook a shepherd's crook.[11] The earliest reference to the phrase is 1380, in John Wycliffe's *Controversial Tracts*, when he writes

'...compellen men to bie alle þis wiþ hok or crok...' ('...compel men to buy all these with hook or crook...') The reference may, however, be even older than that and relate, instead, to ideas about the devil: a thirteenth-century manuscript, *The Sayings of Saint Bernard*, which sits in the Bodleian Library, Oxford, gives a stark warning about Satan, who was often depicted with hands as crooks or hooks:

He would have your heart's blood;
Beware of his hook!
Do now as I have told you,
And all three should be vanquished
With their own crook.

John Ray's *A Collection of English Proverbs* from 1678 throws up some wonderfully antiquated ovine catchphrases, the meaning of which isn't always clear to modern readers. 'Better be a shrew then a sheep', meant better to be a battleaxe than a meek wife; 'Where every hand fleeceth the sheep goes naked' was a warning about collective avarice; 'he whose sheep die of the rot, saves the skins and wool' is a rather gruesome equivalent of 'every cloud has a silver lining'; and the particularly descriptive 'As hasty as a sheep, so soon as the tail is up the turd is out' probably refers to doing something with indecent haste.

Many of these seventeenth-century words of wisdom in Ray's book appeared alongside foreign versions of the phrases; sheep sayings clearly work across borders. The self-explanatory 'He that makes himself a sheep, shall be eaten by the wolf', for example, has versions in both Italian ('*Chi pecora si fa il lupo la mangia*') and French ('*Qui se fait brebis le loup le mange*').[12]

Another famous phrase 'A wolf in sheep's clothing' – a person who hides vicious intent under a veneer of kindness – has a particularly ancient pedigree. It appears in the New Testament – Matthew 7:15 – as part of Jesus' Sermon on the Mount: the King James Bible declares, 'Beware of false prophets, which come to you in sheep's clothing, but inwardly they are ravening wolves'. All is not lost, however, as they will reveal themselves by their actions – 'by their fruits shall ye know them'.

This phrase is often wrongly described as coming from Aesop's Fables, an older text written in ancient Greece around the end of the sixth century BC, but Aesop's large collection of allegorical stories does include plenty about sheep and wolves and the uncomfortable relationship between them. 'The Dog, the Wolf and the Sheep' is a cautionary tale about bearing false witness – the sheep is falsely accused of stealing by the dog, with the wolf backing up his story. The sheep is found guilty of the crime, but in the end it's the wolf that dies – the moral being that liars get their comeuppance. The tale of 'The Wolf and the Shepherds' is a brilliantly pithy warning about hypocrisy. As retold by Plutarch, 'A wolf seeing some shepherds in a shelter eating a sheep, came near to them and said, "What an uproar you would make if I were doing that!"[13] 'The Wolf and the Lamb' is a rather more depressing tale of tyranny: a wolf, wanting to eat a lamb, justifies it by listing all the things the lamb has done wrong in his short life. The lamb protests his innocence but the wolf eats him anyway, finding other excuses to commit the act. The moral, one suspects, is that a bad person will always find a reason for his actions.

People wanting to commit themselves wholeheartedly to a particular course of action sometimes say: 'Might as well be hanged for a sheep as for a lamb' – the idea being that if you're going to get caught for a crime, you might as well aim for the bigger prize. The saying works without any knowledge of its historical reference, but it clearly comes from a time when one could end up dangling at the end of a noose for even the most minor of offences.

The phrase is already well known by the time it appears in John Ray's book in the seventeenth century: 'As good be hang'd for an old sheep as a young lamb'. At the time Ray was putting pen to paper, there were already fifty crimes in Britain for which a person could be put to death. That number had quadrupled by 1776 and capital offences ranged from the serious, such as murder and high treason, to the downright ludicrous, including forgery, damaging Westminster Bridge, associating with gypsies, cutting down trees, being out at night with a blackened face and robbing a rabbit warren.

Stealing a sheep was also on the list. In reality, whether you were hanged for your crime depended on the mood of the court and how merciful a particular judge was feeling on the day. A news report in the *Stamford Mercury*, Lincolnshire, dated Friday 7 August 1801, shows how fickle the rulings could be:

> John Exton and Ann Baker the two prisoners under sen-tence at Oakham for stealing sheep from Mr. Wyles, of Stretton, were executed on Monday last. They both acknowledged their guilt, and behaved with propriety in their unhappy situations. The man met his fate rather with an appearance of satisfaction than dismay; but the poor woman was much affected. On Friday last three more sheep stealers, named Tyers, Nutt, and Barfield, on the impeachment of the latter, were committed to Oakham gaol [...]

The last person to be hanged for sheep stealing in England was John Clarke, a forty-four-year-old butcher and father of four. He'd been accused of stealing two sheep from a local field, the carcasses of which were discovered in his shop. Clarke went to the gallows insisting that he'd found the sheep wandering along the road, but both judge and jury found him guilty. He was hanged at Lincoln Castle on 19 March 1830. Again, the *Stamford Mercury* was there to report the scene:

The country people had been streaming in from an early hour in the morning and many foolish parents sent or brought with them crowds of children of both sexes under the weak and almost hypocritical pretext of 'giving them a warning', it was too plain that the dreadful preparations had little to impress the greater part of the gaping spectators. Children were throwing oranges or running about the castle ditch. Jokes and levity abounded on all sides and when at length those who were high enough gave notice that the wretched procession might be seen moving across the castle yard the cry of 'they're coming, they're coming' that sounded on all sides was such as might have announced the commencement of a bull baiting, a boxing match or a horse race.

It must have been cold comfort indeed, for Clarke's family, when the sentence of hanging for sheep theft was abolished only two years later.

6

MR AND MRS
BO-PEEP

Shepherd wanted, blasted sheep and the
saving grace of crushed testicles

Eating grass is a convoluted business. In order to take in enough nutrition, sheep will graze for eight to ten hours at a stretch. They scoff quickly, like lunch-box schoolkids, chewing the grass only briefly, before swallowing it down. But then the hard work really starts – after the grass has been in their stomach for about an hour, they regurgitate it back into their mouths and begin carefully chewing each mouthful, up to fifty times, often finding somewhere quiet to sit while they do it. This is 'chewing the cud'.

The cud-chewing habit has consequences for both sheep and people. One is that sheep need large tracts of land and have to be moved on once a pasture is exhausted. The second is that sheep – who spend so much of their time either head down, grazing, or sitting and ruminating, are pretty vulnerable to predators. Any defences that wild sheep did have – such as large horns – were often bred out of domesticated populations either by accident or design. One of the only defence mechanisms sheep have is their ability to flock together, making it trickier for predators to pick off a lone straggler.

Research has shown that different breeds of sheep have different tendencies to flock together. Some, like Merino sheep, like to huddle in one, tight-knit group that stays together at all times. Some breeds, like Southdowns, break off into smaller sub-groups when they're feeding, but come back together when they rest. And some, like Dorset Horns or Scottish Blackfaces, can happily spend most of their time in small groups or even graze by themselves. These different social systems may have formed over the years as a result of habitats – some presenting more of a risk from predators than others – but what's amazing is that sheep tend to stick to their own kind; put a mix of different breeds into a field and – like boys and girls at a school disco – they'll naturally separate off into their own clans.

Either way, our domestication of sheep came with a career opportunity – the new role of shepherd or shepherdess. Someone had to watch over these unruly, wandering assets-on-legs, protect them from thieves, wolves, bears and other predators and lead them to pastures new. From the archaeology it's clearly an ancient profession. Five thousand years ago, while Stone Age farmers were dragging vast megaliths into place at Stonehenge, over in the Middle East, urbanization was already beginning to take hold. Cities had grown up along the Tigris and Euphrates rivers, the wheel and writing had emerged, and both potters and builders were scaling new heights of craft and creativity.

Civilization was racing ahead, thanks in no small part to wealth that was being generated from sheep and wool. One of the earliest pictures we have of a shepherd comes from around this time; a cylinder seal (a sort of personal ID stamp) sitting in the British Museum shows a bearded shepherd, with a stripy robe, carrying a whip and a staff. He's surrounded by the tools of his trade – a sheepdog, a sheep pen and what looks like some rounds of sheep's cheese drying in the sun. It's a little chipped and worn in places, but that's not surprising given it's nearly four thousand years old. But what's clear is that shepherding is already a recognized profession.

Over the millennia, there have been different ways to be a shepherd. The oldest, perhaps, is nomadic herding. These are shepherds constantly on the move, living in small tribal or family groups, who choose not to settle in one place. This type of controlled wandering across landscapes, which are often too dry or desolate to farm, works because the sheep provide everything the transient community needs for its own use – milk, cheese, meat, wool and dung for fuel – and perhaps a little surplus, which can be traded. It's an ancient way of life, from the nomads of the Tibetan plateau to the Bedouins of the Middle Eastern deserts, but one that often clashes with modern borders, urbanization and pressure from governments to lead a settled existence.

Some shepherds are semi-nomadic, living a settled life for part of the year but still pursuing their flocks for long stretches at a time. The Mongolians were, and are, masters of the semi-nomadic existence – a quarter of Mongolia's population still lives as semi-nomadic shepherds – but smaller, less well-known groups are tucked away in remote corners of the globe, quietly continuing a way of life that straddles both worlds.

It's easy to imagine the life of the shepherd as a lonesome, solitary pursuit, but for many semi-nomadic communities, shepherding is a family affair. The Dhangars, in the western Indian state of Maharashtra, for example, travel in small groups – sometimes only a husband and wife with their children, and a hundred or so sheep. Following the path of the southwest monsoon, they criss-cross the arid, rocky land-scape, travelling around 500 miles (800 kilometres) over a nine-month period in search of suitable grazing land.[1]

Transhumant shepherds, on the other hand, also follow the seasons, but usually between the same two permanent settlements – often cool, rich mountain grazing in the warm summer months and back down in the sheltered lowlands for winter (and sometimes an additional, third halfway pasture during the spring). It's a fast disappearing way of life but, until the beginning of the twentieth century, was characteristic of sheep-farming cultures across Southern and Eastern Europe, Asia, Africa, India and parts of America.

Europe's Alps epitomise the tradition – the clanking sheep bells, rugged, high-altitude scenery and lonely shepherds straight from the pages of *Heidi* – but Great Britain also had its own gentle, transhumant tradition. Even after the First World War, for example, Romney Marsh lambs were still moved from the marshes along the Kent coast to the rich uplands of Kent and Sussex, to spend autumn and winter away from home. The ewes stayed behind, able to cope with the scant grazing and diseases which often carried off their young. Come the spring, mums and lambs were reunited.[2]

Shepherds in the Romney Marshes were known as 'lookers' or 'lookerers'. The 'lookering system' grew out of the devastation caused by the Black Death in the Middle Ages, when landowners began buying up vast tracts of depopulated marshland to graze with sheep. Lookers were employed to keep an eye on multiple, large flocks, covering huge distances on foot, and spending long periods away from home in tiny, brick huts called 'Lookers' Huts'. These sparse but sturdy buildings were ideal for lambing and shearing time – a looker could spend weeks on end, holed up in his shelter, relying on family to bring provisions from time to time.

In their heyday, during the eighteenth and nineteenth centuries, there were over three hundred huts dotted around the marshes. Now, only ten or so remain. Oddly, lookers didn't see themselves as shepherds. Romney sheep didn't need close shepherding – they were bred to be hardy, independent creatures – but it was as much a matter of job title; shepherds worked for a single farmer, or kept their own flock, while a looker saw himself more as a vital overseer, keeping a beady eye on the flocks of a handful of farms at once.

Shepherds' huts have, of course, become popular bolt-holes once again. It's remarkable to think that what was once an uncomfortable reality for a working shepherd has become the go-to destination for a luxury break, but there's something undeniably cosy about these mobile, self-sufficient shelters. Just a room on wheels, they provided everything the shepherd could need for his enforced isolation out in the fields.

Alongside lambing and shearing duties, shepherds were also called upon for 'folding'. Before the advent of modern fertilizers, a useful way to enrich fallow land was to call in a shepherd and his flock. Kept in place with wooden or hazel hurdles, the sheep were encouraged to graze the land for a few weeks or given supplementary feed. As they ate, their manure enriched the ground, often turning previously poor land into productive acreage. Indeed, for some areas, without the shepherd and sheep, there would have been no farming at all; folding, for example, was pivotal to the success of English chalkland farming in the eighteenth century. Counties such as Hampshire, Wiltshire, Dorset and Berkshire – which often suffered from difficult, poor terrain for arable farmers – were reliant on sheep poo to raise the fertility of the downland soil. Without the flocks of sheep constantly treading in and feeding the soil with their manure, the farmland would have soon become exhausted and useless for arable crops.[3]

We know what early shepherds' huts looked like thanks to religious paintings. Shepherds, being key players in the Christian story, often make a centre-stage appearance in medieval art. In gloriously illuminated documents of scenes such as the 'Annunciation to the Shepherds', you don't have to look too hard to find examples of their huts tucked away in the background.

These medieval examples are sometimes windowless, wooden boxes with just enough room for the shepherd to lie down. Such two-wheel carriages would have needed to be pulled into place by draught animals and propped up for stability, but the concept was a winner. As late as the 1950s charming postcards from France show this shallow hut still in use in rural communities, often with a shepherd helpfully reclining inside.

Shepherds' huts only really suit flat, gentle terrain, however. Many hill and mountainside shepherds built small permanent structures – rather like the Lookers' Huts of the Romney Marshes – where they could take shelter, keep young lambs and, sometimes, make and store cheese. *Orris*, in the Pyrenees, for example, were traditional summer mountain huts built by hand, often with stone cleared from the fields to make way for pasture. Sometimes isolated, sometimes grouped in little hamlets, these tiny buildings allowed transhumant herders to rest their heads, milk their sheep and keep vulnerable animals safe overnight. Similar huts pop up all over mountainous regions of Europe, each with its own vernacular name: *kažun* in Croatia, *tholos* in southern Italy, *pinetta* in Sardinia and *borie* in Provence.

Back to our mobile shepherds' huts: other medieval paintings show four-wheel versions, some with a hinged door at the front and shutters on the sides so the shepherd could watch his flock even if the lashing rain forced him inside. It's this second type of shepherds' hut that most of us are familiar with today. By the nineteenth century, a typical interior would include a raised bed, with a caged space underneath for poorly or injured lambs (called a lamb rack). There would have been just enough room for a folding table, perhaps, a small iron stove and a wall cupboard for sheep 'remedies', often little more than a bottle of whisky to revive a sick lamb or, more likely, a weary shepherd.

You can't think of shepherds without also picturing their 'smocks', the loose, flowing dress of the eighteenth- and nineteenth-century agricultural labourer. The garment has a long history: the *Luttrell Psalter*, which was written and illuminated between 1325 and 1340, shows lively scenes of rustic life on a Lincolnshire estate; in it, shepherds clearly wear smock-like clothes, and by the early 1700s, the smock was the standard working uniform for the herder and farmer.

Plain smocks were worn for everyday but men would also have fancier smocks for Sunday Best and celebrations.

Smocks were usually made from cotton or linen, mostly naturally plain coloured but sometimes dyed in the local tradition, such as 'Nottingham blue' or 'East Anglia green'. The smocked stitches, far from being a design frippery, were integral to the garment's flexibility and strength: smocking the fabric – which involved gathering the cloth into tiny folds – not only allowed for a degree of stretch but it also helped reinforce the garment at the wrists, chest and shoulders, the areas which got the most wear.

The Industrial Revolution spelled the end of the smock, however. Shepherds and other rural workers, who left the land to find work in the newly opened factories, quickly discovered that loose clothing and mill machinery made a lethal combination. Elizabeth Gaskell's *North and South*, written in 1855, even mentions the problem; the novel's chief protagonist, Margaret Hale, who has travelled from the serenity of the rural south to a grim, industrializing mill town in the north, is immediately struck by the difference in people's clothes: 'The colours looked grayer – more enduring, not so gay and pretty. There were no smock-frocks, even among the country folk; they retarded motion, and were apt to catch on machinery, and so the habit of wearing them had died out.'[4]

By the end of the nineteenth century the shepherd's smock as a utilitarian uniform had all but disappeared, save for in the odd pocket of English countryside. As rural traditions waned, an increasingly urban population became nostalgic for a lost, and to a large extent imagined, world of handicrafts and pastoral life, epitomised by the Arts and Crafts movement and the illustrations of Kate Greenaway and Walter Crane; smocked clothing, which many associated with simple, honest rural living, would make an unlikely leap from butch, sheep handler's overall to oh-so-pretty dresses for middle-class women and children.

Out in the field, shepherds were expected to deal with all manner of sheep ailments and problems by themselves. The typical nineteenth-century shepherd might have had a few folk remedies to draw on, such as wrapping birch bark around a sheep's broken leg, or applying a quick smear of home-made 'salve' for sheep skin problems. Medieval recipes for shepherd's salve mention oil and tallow, or tar and butter, but by the eighteenth and nineteenth centuries, toxic ingredients such as mercury or turpentine had crept into the mix.

Turpentine was also used as a remedy for that most feared of ailments – bloat, or 'sheep blast' – the price of gorging one-self on rich pasture or root vegetables. Purgatives like Epsom salts or castor oil were also common remedies but, failing that, 'popping' the inflated sheep was the only option. An early nineteenth-century sheep-rearing guide walks us through the process:

> The shepherd has recourse to the use of his knife in these cases: he plunges it into the left flank, a little below the chine,

and half way between the haunch and the ribs. The gas will rush violently out; the patient will be evidently relieved, and often the immediate inconvenience and danger from the distension of the stomach will entirely cease.[5]

It was a risky business, the initial relief often followed by infection and a slow, agonising death for the unfortunate sheep. From the early 1800s, however, a new invention – the trocar, or 'letting spike' – offered skilled shepherds a slightly more accurate alternative. In Thomas Hardy's novel *Far from the Madding Crowd* (1874), the stoic, heroic shepherd Gabriel Oak comes to the rescue of Bathsheba Everdene, whose flock has accidentally broken into a field of young clover and gorged themselves into life-threatening 'blast'. Things are looking bleak for our heroine – if nothing is done the sheep 'will all die as dead as nits', cries the farmhand. At the last hour, however, Oak saves the day:

Gabriel was already among the turgid, prostrate forms. He had flung off his coat, rolled up his shirt-sleeves, and taken from his pocket the instrument of salvation. It was a small tube or trochar, with a lance passing down the inside; and Gabriel began to use it with a dexterity that would have graced a hospital surgeon. Passing his hand over the sheep's left flank, and selecting the proper point, he punctured the skin and rumen with the lance as it stood in the tube; then he suddenly withdrew the lance, retaining the tube in its place. A current of air rushed up the tube, forcible enough to have extinguished a candle held at the orifice. It has been said that mere ease after torment is delight for a time; and the countenances of these poor creatures expressed it now.

The character of Gabriel Oak is perhaps one of the most famous romantic representations of a shepherd – stable, quiet and loyal, protector and guardian to the innocent. Lamb in one hand, crook in another, the shepherd as an emblem of dependability and trustworthiness has, in fact, featured in both art and literature for hundreds of years – from High Renaissance paintings to William Blake's 'The Shepherd'.

It was an honourable job with high expectations – one treatise on estate management, from the late 1200s, insists a shepherd should be of impeccable character and must not leave his sheep 'to go to fairs, markets or wrestling matches or spend the evenings with friends or go to the tavern'.[6] Another text makes it clear how a shepherd is expected to behave:

It profiteth the lord to have discreet shepherds, watchful and kindly, so that the sheep be not tormented by their wrath but crop their pasture in peace and joy-fulness; for it is a token of the shepherd's kindness if the sheep be not scattered abroad but browse around him in company.

Let him provide himself with a good barkable dog and lie nightly with his sheep.[7]

The honourable shepherd is an ancient metaphor: two thousand years before the birth of Christ, Hammurabi, king of Babylon, called himself 'the shepherd who brings peace'; God in the Jewish, Christian and Muslim faith is often described as the 'good shepherd', leading his flock to safety and protecting them from harm. In fact, herders of all descriptions are used as religious symbols of benign leadership and spiritual gathering, from Govinda the cowherd in Hinduism to the ox herder in the Buddhist parable. Many world religions emerged at the same time that sheep domestication and other forms of herding were also evolving and growing; ancient congregations would have understood pastoral references and metaphors as reflections of their daily life.

The Bible, however, draws on the metaphorical potential of sheep and sheep-rearing to an extraordinary degree. Mentions of sheep, lambs, flocks that need guidance, shepherds, and nourishing pastures are everywhere – even the shepherd's crook becomes a widely accepted 'badge of office' in the church.[8] In the Old Testament, Israel is a flock under the care of God, while in the New Testament, Jesus' parable of the Good Shepherd elegantly explains his purpose, to lead his flock, protect them, gather in the wayward, risk his life against predators, and carry the helpless lambs.

The shepherd's lowly, humble reputation becomes the motif of the reluctant but worthy leader – David's victory over Goliath with just a shepherd's slingshot speaks volumes – and it seems obscurity and lack of overarching ambition were the perfect personality traits for greatness. Jesus is also referred to in the Gospel of John as the *Agnus Dei* or 'Lamb of God who takes away the sins of the world'. The choice of a lamb is fascinating and its symbolism wouldn't have gone unnoticed by early Christian audiences.

Animal sacrifices, especially sheep, are littered throughout the Old Testament:

'You shall also offer one male goat for a sin offering and two male lambs one year old for a sacrifice of peace offerings.' (Leviticus 23:19)

'But if he brings a lamb as his offering for a sin offering, he shall bring it, a female without defect.' (Leviticus 4:32)

'Then you shall take the other ram, and Aaron and his sons shall lay their hands on the head of the ram. You shall slaughter the ram, and take some of its blood and put it on the lobe of Aaron's right ear and on the lobes of his sons' right ears and on the thumbs of their right hands and on the big toes of their right feet, and sprinkle the rest of the blood around on the altar.' (Exodus 29:19-22)

These sacrificial offerings were a way of asking for forgiveness, the act of destruction a 'gift' to make things right with God. But the choice of animal was hugely significant. Lambs or sheep 'without defects' would have been the ultimate symbol of purity and cleanliness. Priests had to be blemish-free as well. It's an idea older than the Bible itself – the requirement that both holy men and the objects of their sacrifice had to be perfect – and appears across Egyptian, Mesopotamian, Greek and Roman cultures.

Blemishes were viewed as a direct affront to God – priests who displayed any of the following ailments would have been barred from performing sacrificial duties: *ivver (iwwer)* – blindness; *pisse'ah* – one injured in the thigh; *harum* – a man whose nose is sunk in between his eyes; *sarua* – hands or feet of unequal length; *gibben* – overly long eyebrows; *tevallul* – cataracts; *garav* – dermatitis; *yallefet* – ringworm; and *mero'ah ashekh* – crushed testicle.

Sheep had to pass a similar body check – candidates for sacrifice couldn't be blind or have skin defects, broken or uneven limbs, weird feet or damaged testes.[9] Any sheep less than flawless would have been sent back to the field. The framing of Jesus as the perfect, unsullied 'Lamb of God', who must be sacrificed to save mankind, therefore makes sense if you have the backstory, as ancient readers would have done.

In most literature and art, throughout the centuries, shepherds are depicted as men. But in reality, shepherding was often a woman or girl's job. Varro, writing at the height of the Roman Empire, notes: '... those who range the trails should be sturdier than those on the farm who go back to the steading every day. Thus on the range you may see young men, usually armed, while on the farm not only boys but even girls tend the flocks.'[10]

It also wasn't unusual for men and women to shepherd together, as couples, especially those who spent months away at a time. There are some glorious medieval illustrations of men and women shepherding alongside each other, shearing together, and celebrating seasonal festivities, with little of the self-conscious gender separation that often accompanies practical work. Co-shepherding had been a functional part of the countryside for centuries; our Roman writer, Varro, notes how the women who accompany their partners in the shepherding life have to be as tough as the men, carrying out their fair share of the physical work while giving birth and child-rearing in remote 'mountain valleys and wooded lands' with little outside support:

Such women should, however, be strong and not ill-looking. In many places they are not inferior to the men at work, as may be seen here and there in Illyricum [western Balkans], being able either to tend the herd, or carry firewood and cook the food, or to keep things in order in their huts. As to feeding their young, I merely remark that in most cases they suckle them as well as bear them.

The image of the shepherdess is one that has fascinated writers and painters for centuries. It's an interesting idea to unpick. These tough, independent women have, over the years, offered a welcome change from the limited representations of what constitutes suitable 'women's work'. Films and books about these indomitable females still strike a chord with audiences, from the award-winning 2015 Indian documentary film *The Shepherdess of the Glaciers*, about one woman's quiet determination to lead her 300-strong flock across the Himalayan Plateau, to the 'Yorkshire Shepherdess' Amanda Owen, with her no-nonsense, hard graft approach to hill farming while raising nine children. The notion of the noble, tough, isolated woman is a powerful antidote to the familiar tropes about women's roles in society.

Not all representations are as positive as these, however. In the lavish *Shepherd and Shepherdess Making Music*, a sixteenth-century Dutch tapestry in the Metropolitan Museum of Art, New York, a couple are shown entertaining themselves with music, as the sheep graze idly in the meadowed background. It would be a scene of perfect bucolic harmony, if it wasn't for the embroidered song lyrics. The shepherdess trills: 'Let's sing, on the grass, with your bagpipe, double a tune for two', only for her lover to respond 'When she sings her voice is fair: but I do the work.'

From the sixteenth century onwards, however, the image of the shepherdess at the centre of an idyllic landscape became an increasingly prominent one in poetry, art and literature. Pastoral writing was nothing new – Virgil's *Georgics* and *Eclogues* had described a world filled with nymphs and shepherds, living simple, quixotic lives as long ago as the first century BC – but big literary hits such as Jacopo Sannazaro's poem *Arcadia* (1480) and Marlowe's 'The Passionate Shepherd to His Love' (1599) cemented the idea of the rustic idyll and its attractively unsophisticated inhabitants.

Both shepherds and shepherdesses became nostalgic symbols of a heady combination of honest toil and rustic pleasures; women sheep herders and peasant girls, in particular, were the very epitome of barefooted health, hard work and, more often than not, buxom sexuality. It's no coincidence, for example, that many representations of Joan of Arc, a figure celebrated for her humble roots, independent-mindedness and courage, depict her as a beautiful but poor shepherdess, despite the fact that she was the daughter of a reasonably comfortable farming family and probably never herself herded sheep.[11]

Interestingly, the nursery rhyme 'Little Bo-Peep' is probably one of the few representations of shepherdesses that paint the female sheep herder as being as absent-minded and feeble as her flock:

Little Bo-Peep has lost her sheep,
And doesn't know where to find them;

leave them alone, And they'll come home,
wagging their tails behind them.

In 1784, English lawyer and antiquarian Joseph Ritson* compiled a book of well-known nursery rhymes rather splendidly titled *Gammer Gurton's Garland; or, The Nursery Parnassus: a choice collection of pretty songs and verses, for the amusement of all little good children who can neither read nor run.* Little Bo-Peep gets a mention. This, and another work from 1806, called *Critical Comments on the Bo-Peepeid*, suggest the rhyme had been around for some time.[12]

The name 'Bo-Peep' had been in use since at least the fourteenth century, to describe the baby game we would now call 'peek-a-boo'. A 1364 reference mentions one unfortunate woman, punished for serving short measures of ale, having to 'play bo pepe thorowe a pillery',[13] while an Elizabethan ballad first links the ideas of Bo-Peep and sheep, 300 years before

* Ritson was a fascinating man. Born into humble circumstances in Durham in 1752, he made his way to London to become a successful conveyancer in his early twenties. In his spare time, he passionately consumed local poetry, ballads and folklore – subjects often ignored by the literary world – and subsequently published dozens of books on fairy tales, legends and historical romances, including *Gammer Gurton's Garland*. For all his interest in children's literature and stories, Ritson was also well known for his furious and unpredictable temper, sympathies with the French Revolution and vegetarian activism. In his mid-forties, however, Ritson started showing the early signs of mental illness. In 1803, at the age of fifty-one, he barricaded himself into his chambers at Gray's Inn, set fire to his manuscripts, and was eventually removed to a friend's house in Hoxton, where he died impoverished and insane.

the rhyme became a nursery favourite: 'Halfe England ys nowght now but shepe, In every corner they play boe-pepe.'[14] If only Little Bo-Peep had had a trusty sheepdog by her side, she might not have got into such a pickle in the first place.

7

DOGS AND DROVERS

Come By, Corgis and the Bank of Black Sheep

We may have sheep to thank for man's best friend – the dog. While we still haven't pinned down the exact date that wolves rolled over to have their tummies tickled, it looks as if the development of sheep herding and the need for canine assistance went hand in hand. Far from sleeping on the sofa and going for the occasional walk, early domesticated dogs would have enjoyed an uneasy truce with their human companions; some would have been used for hunting, others to guard the settlements. Some dogs were kept as mobile waste disposal units, cleaning up and scavenging scraps around the camp, while others were deployed for combat or dog fights. It also wasn't unusual for dogs to find their way onto the menu – remains from Iron Age sites, for example, have shown evidence that adult dog meat and the heads of both puppies and fully grown dogs were eaten grilled or roasted.[1]

The archaeology suggests that domesticated dogs first appeared sometime between 12,000 and 20,000 years ago. Around 6,000 to 10,000 years ago we start to see the emergence of different types and sizes of dogs, including small breeds and new colours of coat. Dogs bred for two roles in particular, however, proved especially useful to our ancestors – livestock guardians and herding dogs. Livestock guardians were the bouncers of the dog breed world. One of the most famous was the *molosser*, a solid slab of a dog favoured by the ancient Assyrians and Greeks and one of the first explicitly mentioned as sheep sentinels. In the fourth century BC Aristotle, in his *History of Animals*, sings their praises:

> Of the Molossian breed of dogs, such as are employed in the chase are pretty much the same as those elsewhere; but sheep-dogs of this breed are superior to the others in size, and in the courage with which they face the attacks of wild animals. Dogs that are born of a mixed breed between these two kinds are remarkable for courage and endurance of hard labour.[2]

These were big, brutish dogs, often with white fur so the shepherd could see the dog in poor light and distinguish it from other animals at a distance. Roman livestock guardian dogs wore spectacular spiked metal collars, something that wouldn't look out of place on Dennis the Menace's dog Gnasher, from *The Beano*; far from being for show, these collars gave guardian dogs a fighting chance in a head-to-head battle – wolves and other wild predators often going for the neck in an attack.

Not everyone needed such a big, muscly dog, however. Most people at this time would have owned only a few sheep and practised mixed farming on a modest scale. And large dogs such as molossers would have had hearty appetites, which would have put them beyond the means of most families. Livestock guardian dogs were only needed if two conditions were met: one was the practice of large-scale transhumant or nomadic sheep farming, and the other was the presence of a genuine threat from carnivorous predators such as bears, wolves, lions, leopards and cheetahs, depending on where you lived.

In the few parts of the world where large carnivores still prey on sheep, herders often rely on livestock guardians. In Mongolia, for example, Bankhar dogs are used protect flocks (and other herds) from the last few remaining snow leopards and wolves that roam the wilderness. In England, by contrast, thanks to our consistent and ruthless persecution of large predators, the lynx had gone by the end of Roman rule, brown bears had disappeared before the Norman Conquest, and wolves had all but vanished by 1500; indeed in 1570, the physician John Caius (one of the founders of Gonville and Caius College, Cambridge) wrote: 'Our shepherdes dogge is not huge, vaste, and bigge, but of an indifferent stature and growth, because it has not to deale with the bloudthyrsty wolf, sythence there be none in England.'[3]

While the job description of the livestock guardian could be summed up as a 'shepherd's killer companion', the herding dog required an entirely different skill set. Rather than defend, the herding dog's aim was to drive sheep in a particular direction, either by barking, body language, nips or touches of the muzzle. And, unlike livestock guardians, the history of the herding dog is a bit of a mystery.

What's interesting is that, although the livestock guardian dog is the more aggressive of the two types of dog, it is the sheepdog who's encouraged to behave more like his wolf cousin. Livestock guardians have had their instinct to devour the sheep bred out of them, but the skill of the shepherd is to get a herding dog to mimic his natural instinct to hunt and to separate out or gather together the sheep.

It's also curious that the development of the herding dog may have come much later than the livestock guardian. While there are mentions of 'sheepdogs' in Columella's first-century AD work *De Re Rustica*, they are not in a form we would recognize – these kinds of dogs were used to chase after wolves, or pursue predators that had taken a sheep, and so were bred to be long, slim, fast and strong,[4] but there's no hint of the trained, biddable sheepdog we know today. Columella does, however, suggest the idea of using short names for dogs, to make sure they responded quickly to their owner's commands – his favourites included Ferox (Fierce), Celer (Speedy), Lupa (Wolf) and Tigris (Tiger).[5] It's no coincidence that one of the world's oldest dog names – Fido – roughly translates from ancient Latin to 'Faithful' or 'Trusty'.

While no one knows who 'invented' the first sheepdog there are plenty of candidates for early breeds, each emerging independently around the world. The Tibetan terrier and Hungarian Puli, for example, both probably share an ancient rootstock with a small herding dog first developed by the Cuman people of Western China sometime before the ninth century AD. The Vikings also had their own version of sheepdogs; the Norwegian Buhund is one of the oldest Nordic breeds, the name roughly translating to 'homestead dog'. Its early origins are lost in time, but by the end of the ninth century the Vikings had introduced their sheep-herding Buhunds to Iceland, Shetland and Greenland, where descendants of those dogs still exist. A genetic study also found that the German shepherd, the French *Berger Picard*, and five different Italian herding breeds, including the *cane da pastore di Oropa* and *cane toccatore*, also share a common lineage.[6]

It's difficult to know what these early sheepdogs actually did. The word *toccatore* (which comes from the Italian *toccare* - to touch) gives us a clue, as does another name for the same type of breed - 'paratore dogs' - *paratore* in Vulgar Latin means 'to push forward' - but early medieval writing on sheepdogs suggests that the relationship wasn't perhaps as involved and mutual as we see in later breeds. In 1379 the Frenchman Jean de Brie, in *Le Bon Berger* (The Good Shepherd) - one of the earliest 'how to' books - suggests that a shepherd's dog should be trained to grab sheep only by the ear and that it would learn to follow its master by having its jaw and front feet rubbed with bacon rind.[7]

By the 1700s, however, the value of a well-trained dog was apparent, reflected in practical farming guides of the time; the eighteenth-century English farmer and agricultural writer William Ellis was struck by one particularly obedient, intelligent sheepdog: 'This Dog was so well broke that he would go before a Flock, round it, side it, or keep behind it, and this nearer or farther off, at the Word of Command...'[8] Ellis even adds, sweetly, 'this shepherd set his love so much on his dog, that if anyone struck it hard, he has been seen to cry.'

Perhaps the most iconic of all sheepdogs, however, is the Border collie. When the Romans came to England in the first century AD, they brought their large, heavy-boned dogs with them. Relatives of these tough, hard-working herding dogs may have bred with spitz-type dogs brought by the Vikings centuries later, to produce an agile, rugged dog perfectly equipped to work the rocky hills of the Scottish and Welsh borders, hence the name. The 'collie' bit is harder to work out – one thought is that it refers to their coal-black colouring (a *colley* is both a rural name for a sheep with a black face and legs and a dialect word for blackbird).

As soon as people began to congregate in towns, a problem reared its head. If you can't live near your food source, the food source has to be brought to you. And so began the role of the drover, the person whose job it was to drive livestock belonging to farmers and landholders huge distances to urban markets. From the eleventh century to the coming of the railways in the first half of the nineteenth century, people travelling across Britain were often greeted by the sight of hundreds of sheep, cattle, pigs and geese pouring, like water, from upland hill country into lowland market towns.

The men who drove these animals were the cowboys of their time: tough, well-paid workers, who were often trusted with more than just the welfare of their flock. As regular travellers from country to city, drovers were often asked to carry news, parcels or letters, take on financial commissions, and even chaperone the offspring of wealthy families.

Life on the open road wasn't for everyone, however, and many people viewed the itinerant life of the drover with suspicion. Drovers were often accused of deception, theft and loose morals. William Harrison, writing in 1577, complains 'so many of them are too too lewd'.[9] Sometimes it was difficult to tell between drovers and the wandering poor, or vagabonds, a problem that particularly worried the Elizabethans. During this time – in an attempt to clear up the confusion and 'weed out' any unscrupulous drovers – statutes were passed that limited the profession to those who were married and above the age of thirty (not including hired servants). If the drover met these conditions he could then apply for a licence, at cost, and was required to pay another fee for the privilege of registering with the Clarke of the Peace, who kept a list of all the names and address of legitimate drovers, although contemporary accounts of drovers' drunken, wenching ways once they got into town suggests they weren't always on their best behaviour.

Among the oldest thoroughfares still in existence, drovers' roads shaped the landscape of Britain and many other parts of Europe. Some routes that became drovers' roads had a more ancient history, often dating back to prehistoric times, and many of them continued to be used long after the clatter of hooves had ceased. In Britain, most of the droving roads led from the wild, hilly areas of Scotland, Wales and the West Country towards the growing market towns and cities in the east and south, including London.

Animals were often marched vast distances, and in large numbers. Daniel Defoe, writing in the 1720s, describes livestock being driven the long stretch between Caithness in Scotland to East Anglia, a one-way trek of around six hundred miles (965 kilometres). In North Yorkshire, the Hambleton drove road still exists, part of an ancient route that took beasts from Scotland to market in England; at its height, during the early nineteenth century, up to 100,000 animals were herded south along it every year. Across the country, the drove roads were alive with the constant movement of livestock on the hoof – during the eighteenth century, London's Smithfield Market took in 750,000 sheep and 100,000 cattle from drovers each year.

It's difficult to imagine just what a spectacle the droving

party would have made. Over the noise and clamour of hundreds of animals, drovers walking or riding alongside their charges would shout cries of *'Heiptro Ho! Heiptro Ho!'* to warn locals of their approach and give farmers time to pen up their own animals lest they got swept along in the drive.[10] Dogs trotted alongside, nipping at stragglers and keeping the flocks tightly controlled. A number of breeds were well-suited to the task, including the queen's favourite, the heel-snapping corgi, and the gentle giant, the old English sheepdog. The last of these two sheepdogs used to be called the bob-tail collie. In the eighteenth century, working dogs were exempt from taxation, while pet dogs were taxed. To tell the difference, working dogs, including droving dogs, would have their tails docked or 'bobbed'.

The relationship between drover and dog was a close one, however. Mary Russell Mitford, sketching rural life in the 1820s, described life for both master and mutt:

No man between Salisbury Plain and Smithfield was thought to conduct a flock so skilfully through all the difficulties of lanes and commons, streets and high-roads, as Jack Bint, aided by Jack Bint's famous dog, Watch; for Watch's rough, honest face, black, with a little white about the muzzle, and one white ear, was as well-known at fairs and markets as his master's equally honest and weather-beaten visage [...] Watch being renowned for keeping a flock together better than any shepherd's dog on the road – Jack, for delivering them more punctually, and in better condition. No man had a more thorough knowledge of the proper night stations, where good feed might be procured for his charge, and good liquor for Watch and himself; Watch, like other sheep dogs, being accustomed to live chiefly on bread and beer.[11]

It also wasn't unheard of for drovers' dogs to make their own way home. An account from the 1920s remembers a Welsh drover named Clough and his faithful companion:

> [...] a dog named Carlo with a wonderful ability for cattle-driving. Once when [the drover] was in Kent, after long persuasion he sold his pony to a customer and decided to go home by coach. The pony's saddle was put on Carlo's back with a note attached asking the landlords of the inns where he used to stay to give Carlo food and a resting place and then send him on. Carlo was told to go home, and home he went, calling at every inn where he used to stay with his master. After about a week's journey he reached Llandrillo safely with the saddle on his back.[12]

Not all drovers made it back home. The churchyard in Southam, Warwickshire, for example, has several graves of Welsh drovers who died on route to London, including a Robert Lloyd of Dduallt, who died in 1773 from 'drinking small beer when hot' at the local tavern. But droving wasn't all about the sheep. Drovers were often entrusted with large sums of money; not only cash from the sale of the animals at market, but also rents collected on behalf of landlords and business debts.

Travelling with pockets stuffed with money was a dangerous gamble and made drovers easy targets for thieves and cutthroats, and so an early system of private banks was established along popular routes, especially in Wales. The small scale and idiosyncrasy of these country banks, and others connected with different trades, was reflected in the bank notes they issued. Printed in copperplate script on large, thin sheets of paper, with details such as the date of issue and partner's signature often added by hand, these characterful notes often advertised and celebrated the industry they represented: sailing ships for banks in coastal areas; ploughs, cattle or sheep for farming areas; tin-mining in Cornwall; cider-making in Herefordshire; and sheep-shearing in Whitby. The drovers' bank, the Aberystwyth & Tregaron, had black sheep on its notes, the number of sheep denoting the number of pounds, leading to locals calling it the '*Banc y Ddafad Ddu*' or 'Bank of the Black Sheep'.

Drovers also acted as chaperones or guardians. Journeying alone was a perilous business, so some people took the opportunity to travel to town under the protection of the drover. Sons of wealthy merchants and landowners would tag alongside a droving party, partly for protection and partly for the adventure. It wasn't usually seen as a 'suitable' journey for a woman, but we know of at least one – Jane Evans, from Ty'nywaun, Carmarthenshire – who, in the mid-nineteenth century, travelled with drovers all the way from rural Wales to London, in order to join up with nurses heading for Balaclava and the Crimean War.[13]

While dogs and drovers worked hard to keep a flock together, bellwether sheep would often help keep their own kind in step. Bellwethers were, and are, male sheep trained to lead the flock – the name comes from *wether* (the Middle English word for a castrated ram) and *bell* (the sheep would wear a bell around its neck so it could be heard even when out of sight). Treated differently from the rest of the flock, bell-wethers were raised and fed by hand, and would tamely follow the shepherd or drover, leading the rest of sheep in what-ever direction was needed. Abattoirs in the early twentieth century often employed bellwethers to lead flocks of sheep calmly to their slaughter – these unwitting accomplices to the meat trade became known as 'Judas sheep'. A 1921 copy of the *Seattle Daily Times* notes:

One of the very necessary features of every packing house is the 'Judas', an animal trained to walk up the chutes leading to the killing room and lead others of his kind to their doom. There have been 'Judas' steer; 'Judas' sheep, and 'Judas' hogs, which lived by betraying their kind.[14]

Bellwethering was, however, an ancient practice. Aristotle, for example, writes of every flock having a bellwether and it answering to its own name. It continued throughout the medieval period; few accounts exist from this time, but one rare example comes from the drover to King Edward II, who describes a rag-tag band of men and boys making slow progress leading sheep and other animals from Lincolnshire to Yorkshire, to stock up land belonging to the crown:

John the barber, the valet in question, took [...] 313 ewes, to which he assigned a master shepherd at two pence and two boys at three pence a day [...] and 272 lambs and one bellwether to which again he assigned two boys at the same wage. On Friday, May 13th, this miscellaneous herd set out on a progress of nearly 130 miles to Tadcaster in south Yorkshire, where it was to be broken up for the stocking of various royal manors. It covered the first 12 miles, from Sutton to Spalding, in two days, the second 12 miles, from Spalding to Kirton in Holland, in one day, and the 15 miles from Kirton to Bolingbroke in two days, on the first of which John the barber hired twelve cross boys to chase the said animals through the town of Boston.[15]

The word bellwether is still in common use, but not with its original meaning. Now a term thrown around the floors of stock exchanges, it's used to mean a share or company that indicates the future performance of the economy, a harbinger of financial markets. A bellwether can also mean a trendsetter. Only in the English language could it be a compliment to be compared to a castrated ram.

Drovers' roads haven't just shaped the landscape of Britain. Spain has a largest network of drove roads anywhere in Europe, some 78,000 miles (125,000 kilometres) of what are called *vias pecuarias*. Some have been in use since Neolithic times, when hunter-gatherers followed the migratory routes of wild deer, sheep and ox as they travelled from their winter valley grazing to the cooler, summer pastures in the mountains. Unlike Britain, where drove roads were used to take sheep to market, the drove roads of Spain were, and still are, transhumant tracks, for moving sheep between areas of seasonal grazing. The numbers of animals involved were, at one time, staggering: between the eleventh and seventeenth centuries, around 5 million sheep, mostly Merino sheep bred for wool, were moved every year along the *vias pecuarias*.

By the thirteenth century, the Spanish kingdoms had recognized the economic importance of the drove roads and brought them under royal legal protection. The freedom of movement which these drove roads allow is still integral to livestock breeding in Spain; in recent years laws have been passed to protect the *via pecuarias* and the rights of the drovers, even when they clash with the demands of modern city living. Every year in Madrid, for example, large flocks of sheep are still walked through the city streets, not only as a reminder of historic traditions but because the drove roads always went that way. Madrid started life as a market town along the route of migrating livestock – in fact many cities and towns, both in Spain and other parts of Europe, including Britain, sprang up along these ancient sheep roads, providing food, drink, shelter and markets for drovers and their flocks.

In Australia, the vast network of drovers' roads is nick-named the 'long paddock' and covers much of the nation's vast, unpopulated interior. These 200-year-old 'stock routes', as they're known across Australia, were initially set up before the advent of the railway, to allow vast numbers of livestock to move across the country, hugging watering holes, river systems and existing Aboriginal trails. By the early twentieth century the government had started to install purpose-built watering points, each designed to be no more than a day's droving from each other. Queensland has one of the last fully functioning historic droving roads, which stretches along an almost unimaginable 44,740 miles (72,000 kilometres) of track and covers a region of roughly 2.6 million hectares (26,000 square kilometres).[16] Drovers still pay a peppercorn fee to use the route – two cents per kilometre – but must agree to travel at least 9.5 kilometres a day with their livestock; this not only encourages the drovers and their horses to keep a reasonable pace but also stops the animals from overgrazing as they make their way to market.

Perhaps the most famous destination, when it comes to sheep, was London's Smithfield. It was the final stopping point for many of the drovers and their flocks, a place that, for more than a thousand years, has been a busy hub of livestock trading. Smithfield wasn't unused to baying crowds – as well as being a hectic livestock market, in its long life it has also been a popular venue for jousting, summer fairs and public executions. Famous radicals and criminals who breathed their last breath at the site of the sheep market include the Scottish national hero William Wallace, subject of the film *Braveheart*, who was hanged, drawn and quartered here in 1305, and Richard Rouse, the Bishop of Rochester's cook, who was publicly boiled alive in 1531 for poisoning several members of the bishops' household.

In 1174, a clerk of Thomas Becket, Archbishop of Canterbury, described Smithfield as 'a smooth field where every Friday there is a celebrated rendezvous of fine horses to be traded, and in another quarter are placed vendibles of the peasant, swine with their deep flanks, and cows and oxen of immense bulk'.[17] By the mid-1800s, however, chaos reigned and over 1.5 million sheep came, often stampeding, to join the market every year. *The Farmer's Magazine* from 1848 describes the scene in grim detail:

In the course of a year 220,000 head of cattle and 1,500,000 sheep are violently forced into an area of five acres, in the very heart of London, through its narrowest and most crowded thoroughfares; and are there sold, and there slaughtered, in the dark and undrained cellars, stables, and outhouses adjoining. The inhabitants and shopkeepers, on the line of march taken by these herds and flocks, are weekly righted from their propriety by the transit of 4,000 oxen and 30,000 sheep, that are hurried along by reckless drovers, and maddened by savage dogs.

These claims might sound overblown if it wasn't for dozens of other reports, each painting a picture of a grisly, dung-smeared and overcrowded 'aggregation of edible quadrupeds'.[18] Charles Dickens, in *Oliver Twist*, trumps them all, however, with his nightmarish vision:

It was market morning. The ground was covered nearly ankle deep with filth and mire; and a thick steam perpetually rising from the reeking bodies of the cattle, and mingling with the fog, which seemed to rest upon the chimney tops, hung heavily above [...] Countrymen, butchers, drovers, hawkers, boys, thieves, idlers, and vagabonds of every low grade, were mingled together in a dense mass: the whistling of drovers, the barking of dogs, the bellowing and plunging of beasts, the bleating of sheep, and the grunting and squealing of pigs; the cries of hawkers, the shouts, oaths, and quarrelling on all sides, the ringing of bells, and the roar of voices that issued from every public house; the crowding, pushing, driving, beating, whooping and yelling; the hideous and discordant din that resounded from every corner of the market; and the unwashed, unshaven, squalid, and dirty figures constantly running to and fro, and bursting in and out of the throng, rendered it a stunning and bewildering scene which quite confused the senses.

Something had to be done. An Act of Parliament forced the livestock market to be moved to new open ground in Islington in the 1850s, while London worked out what to do with the old site. Sir Horace Jones, architect to the City of London, was tasked with designing a building that would deal only in wholesale meat, rather than live animals. He outdid himself. Work on the Central Market – now a Grade II listed Italianate gem – was finally completed in 1868 and triumphantly declared a 'cathedral of meat'. Jones went on to design Billingsgate Fish Market, Leadenhall Market and, most famously, Tower Bridge. The future for Smithfield, however, hangs in the balance. Plans are afoot to move Smithfield to the fringes of the capital, to join up with Billingsgate and New Spitalfields fruit and vegetable market in a new, vast multi-market site. A millennium of sheep and meat trading on the same 'smooth field' may soon face the chop.

8

SCOURING AND SPINNING

Fairies, fleece grease and extra soft loo roll

In the 1850s, a young draper named Thomas Burberry ran a small clothing shop in the centre of Basingstoke. One day, or so the story goes, Thomas was chatting with one of his regular customers, a local shepherd who bought his smocks at the shop. Thomas was intrigued by the fact that, after the shepherd wore his smocks for a while, the fabric seemed to become water-resistant. The shepherd told Thomas that his smock often absorbed some of the grease that came off the wool when the sheep were being handled or dipped. Could it be this, thought Burberry, that helped the smock repel moisture?

Burberry began to research and experiment with different fabrics, desperate to come up with a material that was both lightweight and comfortable but also breathable and hard-wearing. Sheep's grease, or 'lanolin', proved the missing magic ingredient, the substance that could transform everyday fabric into something remarkable. The cloth Burberry invented and patented – called 'gabardine' after the long, loose outdoor cloaks worn in the Middle Ages – proved a hit, and was the perfect fabric for outdoor coats, military gear and explorers' clothing. Burberry's all-weather cloth protected polar explorers such as Roald Amundsen, Robert Scott and Ernest Shackleton on their perilous Antarctic journeys and was used to make over half a million trench coats for British 'Tommies' in the First World War. How deliciously ironic that Burberry, now a luxury fashion brand, started life with a shepherd, a smock and a liberal smearing of sheep's grease.

Burberry's stroke of genius was his recognition that lanolin is a remarkable substance. Produced by the sebaceous glands in the skin, its purpose is to coat the wool fibres, giving both the skin and the fleece an extra layer of protection against the elements – a kind of sunscreen for sheep. To get lanolin from freshly shorn wool, you need to wash it in hot water – a process known as *scouring* – and then skim the grease off the surface.

Along with its amazing waterproofing qualities, lanolin is also an exceptional emollient for softening the skin, and it's been used in cosmetic and cures for thousands of years. The Greek physician Dioscorides mentions the softening properties of lanolin as early as the first century AD. Describing a kind of poultice made from wool, he writes:

> The best, unwashed wool is softest, like that from the neck and from the thighs. It is good (moistened in vinegar and oil or wine) as first treatment for wounds, bruises, peeling, black and blue bruises, and broken bones. For it easily

drinks up the liquors into which it is dipped, and by reason of the oesypum [lanolin] that it contains it is softening.[1]

The use of lanolin is mentioned in several early pharma-copoeias, including *Dispensarium Coloniense* of 1565, but it was also a staple ingredient in home-made cures throughout the centuries. Women were often expected to take on much of the routine medical care in the household, pulling ingredients from the garden and making various cures from what was to hand in the kitchen. In the Middle Ages, lanolin was a key ingredient for the home-based healer, along with vinegar, wine and honey.[2] Since it is readily absorbed into the skin, lanolin makes the ideal carrier for other medicinal ingredients, but it also has a slight antiseptic quality, helping skin to heal itself and making it an age-old dermatological treatment for everything from burns and nappy rash to cracked nipples and eczema.

Without sheep's lanolin, we also wouldn't have most of the cosmetics and personal care products we've come to rely on – lip balms, shampoos, conditioners, lotions and many make-up products. Oil of Olay – one of the most famous beauty products to emerge after the Second World War – originally contained lanolin as one of its key ingredients. It was invented in 1952 when the South African chemist Graham Wulff decided to create a face cream for his wife that emulated the properties of a young woman's skin. He struggled to find a name for it, but after messing around with the letters in the word 'lanolin' he came up with name 'Oil of Olay'.

In fact, look a little closer and you find lanolin as a surprise ingredient in the strangest of places: medieval knights would coat their arms and armour with sheep's grease to prevent rust, an anti-corrosion technique that's still employed in engineering and boat-building today; lanolin greases the wheels and cogs of machinery, lubricates brass instruments, softens baseball gloves, creates shoe polish and even pops up in concrete water-proofing products, aircraft glues, conveyor belt wax and extra soft loo paper.

The Romans also knew the magical properties of lanolin, a by-product of their vast wool industry. Wool was *the* major textile during the Roman period, and certain regions became synonymous with fleece production; in Italy, the Po Valley, the Alps, Liguria and Calabria became centres for sheep raising, while Spain, northern Gaul, Greece and Asia Minor also pro-vided important sources of high-quality wool to feed the empire's incessant demand for fine cloth. Different regions became expert at breeding sheep with different coloured wools: northern Italy specialized in pure white wool, Spain produced excellent black and deep brown-red fleeces, while Mallorca exported grey and black raw wool. And while certain regions acquired a reputation for producing high-quality woollen cloth on a large scale, there was also a brisk cottage industry in woollen production, run – in the main – by women.

Sources from both the Greek and Roman periods seem to show a world where *all* women were expected to spin and weave from infancy; the arrival of a baby girl, for example, would be celebrated by hanging streamers of wool from the door post.[3] Most houses would have had a workshop, a room set apart for women of the household – whether it was the wife, children or female slaves – to spin wool ready for weaving. The ability to work wool skilfully was seen as an essential and virtuous skill for women of all backgrounds, from the indentured to the highest born.

To turn wool fibres into thread they were first rolled around a long stick called a *distaff*. This stopped the fibres getting tangled, but the distaff could also be held in one hand, or under the arm, while teasing out the fibres with the other. As you gently pulled the wool fibres from the distaff with your thumb and two fingers to create a thread, a spindle and whorl (a stick with a weight attached) was fastened to the other end of the thread left to dangle, keeping the fibres taut. The spinning motion of the spindle, helped by the weight of the whorl, then twisted the wool fibres into yarn. Pulling the fibres and creating a yarn of any consistency and length was a fine art – skilled spinners were admired for their handiwork. In the admiring words of the Roman poet Ovid:

Nor would the work, when finish'd, please so much,
As, while she wrought, to view each graceful touch

Whether the shapeless wool in balls she wound,
Or with quick motion turn'd the spindle round.[4]

The importance of knowing how to spin carried on well into the medieval period and beyond. Gervase Markham, in his 1623 work, *The English Huswife*, advises:

> Our English housewife, after her knowledge of preserving and feeding her family, must learn also how, out of her own endeavours, she ought to clothe them outwardly and inwardly [...] After your wool is thus mixed [...] you shall then spin it up on great wool wheels, according to the order of good housewifery.

Shakespeare, writing just a few years before Markham, plays with the imagery and meaning of distaffs and spinning. In *Twelfth Night*, Sir Toby Belch taunts Sir Andrew Aguecheek outrageously, describing his hair in mocking terms: 'It hangs like flax on a distaff. And I hope to see a housewife take thee between her legs and spin it off.' What he's really saying – and the audience would have fallen about at the bawdy joke – is that Sir Andrew's hair looks like chaotic, fibrous lump, and his best bet is to sleep with a prostitute and catch a venereal disease that will make it all fall out.

The word 'distaff' also symbolized the female domain, an emblem of women's place in society. In *King Lear*, the ageing monarch's vicious daughter, Goneril, rejects the role of obedient wife and seeks to upset gender norms; upon discovering her husband Albany's reluctance to fight, she claims, 'I must change arms at home, and give the distaff / Into my husband's hands'. Shakespeare's audiences would have been both shocked and thrilled at Goneril's dramatic challenge to her husband's masculinity and her sneering suggestion that he was only fit for domestic duties.

There are a number of medieval depictions of women hitting men with distaffs, the emasculating symbolism not difficult to decipher. In one etching, by the fifteenth-century German printmaker Israhel van Meckenem, a woman forces a man to wind yarn – a task that people would have regarded as 'beneath' men – while thrashing him with her distaff. She's also pulling on what looks like a pair of men's underpants, an early version of the woman subverting her socially ordained role by 'wearing the trousers'.

In Chaucer's *Canterbury Tales*, the Host's wife proposes a reversal of traditional gender roles to express her fury at her husband's failure to defend her honour: 'By corpus bones, I wol have thy kniff, And thou shalt have my distaff and go spynne!' she cries. Images of the enraged, distaff-wielding wife thrashing a timid husband crop up in some unlikely places: in the august surroundings of Westminster Abbey we find a carving on a misericord (hinged oak seat) showing a man having his bare bottom beaten by his wife, apparently for breaking her distaff.

The battle of the sexes is also played out in medieval illustrations of distaffs and jousting, with several showing women charging towards unarmed men, distaffs aloft and ready for a fight. The word 'distaff' is still used today, albeit rarely, as an adjective to describe women's concerns or the mother's side of a family. Female horse races are also called 'distaff races' – thoroughbred fillies and mares can still compete in the 'Breeders' Cup Distaff', held annually at a different racetrack in the United States or Canada.

The idea of the 'woman who spins' provides us with the English word 'spinster', a term that still weighs heavy with negative connotations; but for the Greeks and Romans, far from conjuring up a disapproving image of an unmarried woman, the spinner was the epitome of the idealised *matrona*, or wife of an honourable man. The spinster's work symbolized the 'correct' order of life, where women stayed at home, contributing to the self-sufficiency of the household. In Homer's poems from the time, for example, virtually every woman mentioned – including royalty and goddesses – are involved in spinning or creating cloth in some way.[5]

In fact, spinning forms an integral part of many different mythologies and notions of the cosmos. In Plato's *Republic*, he describes the axis of the universe as a shaft of a spindle; the Greek Fates spin the thread of human life; Theseus finds his way out of the labyrinth using Ariadne's spun thread; in the southwestern United States Navajo culture has its own

'Spider Woman', who taught their ancestors how to spin and weave; and in Inca folklore the fertility goddess Mama Ocllo was said to have passed on the art of spinning to Inca women.

Even children's fairy tales are full of spinning – from bed-time favourites such as *Sleeping Beauty* and *Rumpelstiltskin* to lesser-known folk stories such as the *Habitrot* of the border counties of northern England and southern Scotland or the Czech *Golden Spinning Wheel*. What's common to many of these tales is the positive, almost mystical power of spinning. For many girls, young women, mothers and wives, spinning would have been a valuable source of independent income and a way of boosting the family coffers, while still taking care of children or managing a household. Across European folklore there are dozens of folktales which feature heroines who spin; through their craft they are able to save other characters, lift curses and bring about a happy ending. The spinning is not only a means to an end in these tales, but a powerful metaphor about drawing together separate elements to form a single, unbreakable thread.[6]

Spinning and weaving was also, in European folklore, linked to the world of fairies and magic. Scottish woollen weavers often made offerings of milk to the *loireag*, a Highland fairy specifically responsible for overseeing the making of cloth; *Berchta*, a Germanic winter spirit, was said to have one foot flatter than the other from constantly pounding her spinning wheel; *Domikah*, a Russian household fairy, lived under the floorboards and came out at night to spin; both *Girle Guairle*, an Irish fairy spinner, and *Gwarwyn-a-Throt*, a Welsh fairy spinner and weaver, made clothes for needy families. Of all the activities attributed to fairies, spinning and weaving are the most common. Writing at the end of the seventeenth century, Robert Kirk, minister and witchcraft 'expert', describes the *sidh*, or fairy folk:

> Their women are said to spin very fine, to dye, to tissue, and embroider. But whether it is as manual operation of substantial refined stuffs, with apt and solid instruments, or only curious cob-webs, impalpable rainbows, and a fantastic imitation of the actions of more terrestrial mortals, since it transcended all the senses of the seer to discern whether, I leave to conjecture as I found it.[7]

But why would fairies be linked with wool spinning? As we know, the ancient Greeks had the story of the Fates – the three weaving goddesses who controlled the destiny of mankind. The same tale, slightly tweaked, turns up in various forms throughout history and across different cultures such as the Three Norns in Norse storytelling and the sisters *Deivės Valdytojos* in Baltic folklore. In Roman mythology, the three goddesses were known as the *Parcae* or *Fata* (plural of *fatum*, or 'that which has been spoken'). The word *fata*, over time, became *fae* and *faerie* in Old French, and *fairy* in Middle English.

Fairies, until recently, weren't thought of as benevolent, tutu-clad bringers of tooth-money – they were capricious, otherworldly creatures capable of both help and harm, fickle changers of destiny. So, when we read our children bedtime tales of fairies, we are plugging into a two-thousand-year-old story about the Fates, those wool-spinning mistresses of human destiny.

Wool spinning was also a key part of daily life for Viking women, a reality reflected in much of their mythology. Along with the Three Norns, the Vikings also believed in 'seidr' (from the Old Norse seiðr, meaning 'thread'), a type of magic or shamanism which dealt with fate and the possibility of changing the outcome of events. There were seidr rituals for auspicious occasions – for seeing into the future and bringing good luck, for revealing deeply held secrets, for healing and controlling the weather, for encouraging success in hunts and fishing. But seidr also had a dark side and could be used as a terrible curse – to wish ill or death on a person or a community, to induce disaster and accidents, or to blight the land or set someone on a road to ruin.[8]

Crucially, seidr was seen as 'women's magic', and so it's no coincidence that to perform a ritual, the practitioner held a distaff in her hand, before entering into a trance-like state in order to communicate with the spirit world. Women and spinning were intimately linked but, unlike in Greek and Roman culture, where every woman spun, in the Viking world it was very much the 'middle-class' woman's prerogative. The Old Norse Poem *Rígsþula* – written sometime between the tenth and thirteen centuries – gives us a glimpse of who did what, depending on social class: in it, the slave woman wears old clothes and serves food; the aristocratic woman preens herself and drinks wine; and it is the woman of the yeoman class, the land-owning farmers, who is busy with her spindle and loom.

Archaeological evidence, including more than nine thousand textile fragments, indicate that spinning and weaving was practised at nearly every excavated Norse farm in Iceland and Greenland.[9] Indeed, spindle whorls turn up with pleasing regularity in Viking female burials all over Northern Europe. Women were often buried in their best clothes, with several spindle whorls for company. Quite why, we don't know. One thought is that the spindle whorl was a kind of emblem or talisman of the 'home'. Or perhaps the Vikings thought of the whorl as a woman's tool, a symbol of her domestic power and the perfect offering to keep the deceased occupied in her next life.

Different kinds of spindle whorls turn up in female Viking graves – some plain, some fancy, some made from everyday objects, others from valuable, rare materials. Across the Viking world, women's burials are littered with whorls made from materials as diverse as amber, elk antler, bone, clay, coral, glass, metal, wood, sandstone and slate.[10] Some women's graves have one or two, others have handfuls. The variety of whorls in each grave may have been a display of spinning proficiency - a skilled spinner showing her expertise by being buried with lots of different kinds and weights of whorl which, in life, would have allowed her to spin different kinds of woollen yarn. An apprentice or basic spinner may have had, conversely, only one or two whorls to her name. In death, as in life, a Viking woman's status, wealth and skill could be represented through her physical possessions.

Interestingly, it was a Viking spindle whorl that turned up in L'Anse aux Meadows, Newfoundland, which proved not only that Viking warriors had made the arduous journey from Greenland to the New World at least a thousand years ago, but that their womenfolk came along too. In another twist, recent findings have also exploded the idea that the 'advanced' Vikings must have brought the art of spinning to the native Inuit people. Science has shown that the Inuit were spinning yarn hundreds of years before the Vikings arrived; not only that, but Viking and Inuit spinners may have actually swapped techniques - like a spinning 'bee' - with the Norse women learning how to use hair from other animals such as musk ox, foxes and arctic hares, alongside their own imported sheep.

Indeed, Viking voyages and their colonization of distant lands were only possible because of sheep. Norse ships travelled huge distances from Scandinavia, hugging the coasts of

Europe, and using the lakes and rivers of Russia and Germany to trade with Asian and Arab countries. They also struck out for new lands to settle, plunging into the unknown waters that eventually took them to Iceland, Greenland and, eventually, North America.

While Norsemen were skilled sailors, and terrifying warriors, they wouldn't have survived their great journeys without the wool that made their clothes, bedding and even the sails that carried them overseas, most of which were crafted by women and girls. The packing list for a Viking sailor consisted of clothing mostly made from wool. Apart from their leather oilskins, crew members would have worn tunics, socks, gloves, hats, tunics and cloaks all made from sheep's wool, either woven or *nålebound* (an early form of knitting – see page 149), with maybe a thick woollen rug to snuggle under.

But it was the sail that was the game-changer. Roughly speaking, the Vikings used two kinds of ships. The *langskip*, or longship, was an elongated, flat, narrow vessel built primarily for speed and agility, with multiple oarsmen placed along the entire length of the deck for maximum propulsion. The longships had shallow drafts, perfect for navigating shallow rivers and hugging coastlines, and were light enough to be picked up by the crew and carried over land. This made them ideal for fast and furious beach landings and raids. Other European ships of the time needed deep water or harbours to land – Norse raiders, with their shallow drafts, found they could venture further inland than any of their enemies, strike quickly and then make a quick escape from any shelving beach. For long-distance trade and sea exploration, however, a different kind of vessel was needed. The *knarr*, or trade ship, was the shorter, stockier cousin to the longship. It relied almost entirely on sail-power, only resorting to oars when the winds failed to blow. Crews were also smaller on trade ships; fewer men meant profits were greater when shared out. It also had more space for carrying and collecting goods. With fewer hands on deck to row, however, the sail was pivotal to the success of the *knarr*'s voyage.

Densely woven strips of woollen cloth were sewn together to create vast, billowing brightly coloured sheets that could withstand whatever the North Atlantic could throw at it or, if the weather got really bad, be lowered over the ship and fastened down like a tent to shield the sailors inside. Wool might seem a strange choice for a sail, but the key to its success was in its stretchability. Sailing across the ocean, the *knarr* would have been subject to many a fierce storm or sudden blast of wind; wool, with its almost magical elasticity, resistance to tearing and shock-absorbing qualities, could take it all in its stride. The colours would have been dazzling too – analysis of pollen in a Viking dyer's workshop found a rich variety of plants were used to dye the woollen fabric, from chicory black to flax dodder red, goosefoot root yellow to nettle leaves green.

What's startling is just how much wool would have been needed to create a single sail – Amy Lightfoot, textile researcher and head of the Tømmervik Textile Trust in Hitra, Norway, worked out that to make a sail big enough to power a 98-foot (30-metre) boat, which could carry 60 men, you'd need the fleeces of about 700 sheep. It would also have taken longer, she calculated, to make the sail than to build the actual ship – by about a factor of twenty; based on two people working on the task it would have taken about a fortnight to craft a ship, compared to a year to weave a sail.[11] Meanwhile, Danish researchers working at the Viking Ship Museum in Roskilde, totted up that the entire Viking fleet by AD 1050 would have needed 1.2 million square yards (1 million square metres) of woollen sail cloth, a feat of manufacture only possible with the help of 2 million sheep.[12]

That's sheep farming on a monumental scale, not to mention the extensive web of spinners and weavers needed to transform the raw fleece into woollen cloth. The Vikings needed plenty of land to graze all the sheep required to service their ships' needs and domestic wool demand. There simply wasn't enough grazing on Viking soil. In a self-perpetuating cycle, the more the Vikings pushed ahead, trading, colonizing and plundering the lands they encountered, the more foreign pastureland, it seems, they also needed to capture. What the Vikings couldn't produce themselves, they bought from neighbouring countries. Of all the goods that Britain and Ireland had to offer, for example, the Vikings chose to buy wheat, honey, tin and, crucially, cloth. By the closing years of the tenth century, and into the eleventh, there is evidence of woollen fabric produced in the North Sea region ending up in Norway via Viking trade. The thirteenth-century *Egil's Saga* mentions a ship sailing to England 'to buy woollen cloth and other goods he needed', while King Sverre of Norway is said to have praised all those Englishmen who brought 'wheat and honey, flour and cloth' to his country.[13]

Sheep didn't just contribute the wool for Viking ship sails, they provided tallow to waterproof the sails, salted meat for the journey, a live commodity to trade once they'd arrived, coarse hair to make lightweight rope and fishing line, and a means of making a living if they decided to settle. Sheep also helped to make the longships watertight; their wool – mixed with tar or tallow – was used to stuff the spaces between the wooden planks. And, during the night, rather than sleep at sea, Vikings often pulled their longships up on beaches, where they'd take down the woollen sail and lay it across the ship as a tarpaulin. Or they put up woollen tents on land close to shore.

The survival of ancient Viking breeds of sheep in pockets across Europe gives us a direct link with the past. Viking sheep were smaller and hardier than modern commercial breeds, perfectly suited to difficult terrain and minimum tending. They also naturally shed their wool every year, at least partially, making it likely that Vikings would have rooed or plucked the wool from their sheep rather than attempted to shear them. Many of these breeds still live on in isolated communities or thanks to the work of rare breed trusts. The Norwegian Spælsau, the Icelandic sheep, the Swedish Gute (native to the island of Gotland), the Soay and Hebridean in northwest Scotland, the island sheep of Ouessant, off the northwesternmost point of France, and the Manx Loaghtan from the Isle of Man are living reminders of Norse husbandry, trade and settlement across northwestern Europe more than a thousand years ago.

In Britain, local Cumbrian folklore had long spoken of a link between the famous Herdwick sheep and the Vikings, whose farming and culture left an enduring mark on the history and landscape of the Lake District. But the connection had never been proven. However, thanks to the work of the Sheep Trust, a charity based at the University of York, scientists have shown that Herdwicks possess a primitive genome shared by breeds currently living in Sweden, Finland, Orkney and Iceland. The folklore, it turns out, was right.

9

KNIT FOR VICTORY

The world's oldest socks, workhouses
and how wool helped win the war

In 1914, when English collector John de Monins Johnson was sifting through finds in the Egyptian city of Antinopolis, he was hoping to discover some dazzling examples of ancient papyrus. Imagine his disappointment when he found two dusty old woollen socks instead. And, worse still, they didn't even match.

Dismissed as curiosities at the time, these slightly shabby pieces of footwear are now viewed as spectacular survivors of ancient Romano-Egyptian culture, dating to around AD 100– 400, and the oldest woollen socks ever found. At first textile historians thought they had been knitted, but on closer examination it turned out that they had been created using a much earlier technique – knitting's cooler, much older cousin, known as *nålebinding*.

On the surface, *nålebinding* and knitting produce remarkably similar results, but the techniques aren't quite the same. While knitting uses continuous lengths of wool, two or more needles, and a series of interlocking loops which can be unravelled, *nålebinding* needs only one needle, short lengths of wool and involves 'sewing' the loops together. And, while knitting seems to have been a relatively late developer – around the twelfth century AD – *nålebinding* has a truly ancient pedigree.

The word *nålebinding* translates, in some Scandinavian languages, to 'needle binding' and it's interesting that some of the earliest examples of this technique come from Denmark. At one site, a fishing village called Tybrind Vig that was occupied between 5400 and 4000 BC, fragments of a nålebound fishing net were discovered. The net wasn't made from wool, however, but strands of vegetable fibres; it seems knitting, or at least its predecessor, didn't start with woolly jumpers but our ancestors' unending search for food. A quick glance at knitting's linguistic heritage is also telling: the words 'knit', 'knot' and 'net' are all related – branches from the same archaic Proto-Indo-European root *ned-*, meaning to twist, bind or tie.

Perhaps, given its origins, it's no surprise that the Vikings were expert wool nålebinders. Across Russia, Finland, Norway, Denmark, Sweden and Britain, archaeologists have uncovered woollen clothing, or at least fragments, that suggest the Vikings were whipping up mittens, headwear, trimmings, stockings and, most of all, socks, made from local sheep's wool. One example – the 'Coppergate Sock' – which was found under the yard of a tenth-century wattle building in York, is so perfectly preserved you can even make out the shape of the wearer's foot and the place it was lovingly darned at the heel. About the length of a school ruler, with a dainty pointed toe, it looks as comfortable as any modern-day trainer sock, and yet it represents a key moment in British history, when the north of England fell under Viking rule for over a hundred years.

True knitting – the fast, clackety, two-needled kind – seems to have evolved centuries later, perhaps developing from some of the stitches used in *nålebinding*. We know frustratingly little about its beginnings, but knitting is generally thought to have evolved somewhere in the Middle East, between the sixth and eleventh centuries, from where it wound its way into Spain, via Muslim knitters employed by the royal palaces, and into the rest of Europe. The Victoria and Albert Museum holds the earliest scrap of true knitting ever found – a gorgeous cream and blue stocking from North Africa, made around 1100–1300, during a period of Islamic rule, sporting a Fair Isle pattern that wouldn't look out of place in a Ralph Lauren winter catwalk collection.

By the 1400s, knitted clothing had tangled itself into all sections of European society – from king to clergy, lord to pauper. As a craft, knitting led a double life; on one hand, items of breathtaking skill and intricacy were being made for high-status individuals and institutions – cushion covers, liturgical gloves, wall hangings and so on. Knitting at this level was an occupation regulated by hand-knitting guilds, run for and by men, which laid down strict rules for entry and practice.

The Knitters' Guild in Paris during the 1400s, for example, required an apprentice to serve seven years before he could call himself a 'master craftsman'; the job title could only be bestowed on someone who had proved he could design a pair of smart stockings, gloves, a shirt, a waistcoat, and a carpet, and knit all five items in ten weeks or less.[1] Even if a man achieved the status of master, the guild continued to keep a beady eye on his work, dishing out tough penalties or threatening expulsion for shoddy workmanship. The reputation of the guilds kept standards and, crucially, prices high – Henry VIII of England even boasted that the stockings he wore were hand-knitted by the master craftsmen of Paris.

But it's not the high-status, extravagant wool knitting that has the most interesting story. Knitting, because it's a portable, simple craft that doesn't require any expensive equipment, suited the pockets and time constraints of people working in rural subsistence communities or fishing villages. It was a way for poor neighbourhoods to make their own garments, clothes for their families and, most importantly, a means of earning a few extra pennies to supplement their meagre wages. The denizens of marginal agricultural areas and coastal villages could boost their wages by knitting gloves, caps and stockings, often while carrying out other day-to-day chores or paid work. Shepherds knitted alongside their flocks, for example, fisherwomen while waiting for the catch to come in, market traders while selling their wares. Shetland Museum has the most amazing archive of photographs of crofters, many from the late 1800s; in one, two women lug vast baskets on their backs – called kishies – which they used to collect peat for fuel. As they trudge along, baskets loaded, they're also knitting stockings – a feat that seems almost heroic in its multi-tasking.

Another, from 1939, shows a girl of no more than three or four years of age, seated, knitting. As if it wasn't remarkable enough that a pre-schooler had already grasped the complexities of two-needle knitting, she's also wearing a professional knitting belt or, as Shetlanders would call it, a 'makkin belt', a leather strap worn around the waist into which the end of a double-pointed knitting needle is slotted, so a knitter can work quickly and for long periods of time without getting tired.

Knitting probably arrived in Shetland, via England, sometime during the 1600s. The earliest knitted finds come from a seventeenth-century grave of a young man who was buried with a knitted stocking, gloves, a purse and two caps, and by the beginning of the 1700s the islanders realized they could trade knitted woollen stockings and blankets in exchange for cash or goods from Dutch and German merchants.[2] Here and in other regional communities across the British Isles, people knitted while they walked to market, when they huddled around the evening hearth, or sat aboard sailing boats. Men, women and children would knit at any available opportunity – at home, in the field, on journeys. In 1595 it's estimated that around 100,000 people in England were working in the domestic knitting trade.

For many people, therefore, knitting wool represented more than just a useful craft. From the end of the sixteenth century to well into the nineteenth century, it was the means by which communities could try to weather difficult economic times and keep families afloat. Developments in knitting machinery and the move towards industrialization saw much of the hand-knitting cottage industry slip away in Great Britain by the beginning of the 1800s, although pockets of hand knitting continued into the twentieth century, especially in rural areas such as the Yorkshire Dales where it supplemented sheep farming income.

In George Walker's well-known book *The Costume of Yorkshire* – a 1814 collection of watercolours of the county – we see the 'Wensleydale knitters', a small group of hand knitters clacking away in a market square. Everyone's involved – a man, two women and a small girl – a sight that would have been familiar across much of rural Britain. *The Shepherd of Salisbury Plain* (1795) also mentions the practice of young children going round 'wool-gathering', collecting scraps of fleece that had caught on hedges and fences: 'even the very young children could be usefully employed in gathering the locks of wool found on the bramble bushes and thorns, which wool was carded and spun during the winter evening and made into stockings.' Whether these small but valuable amounts of wool were sold, or kept for the family, every little helped. The phrase 'wool-gathering' had been in common use since the 1500s as a way of describing someone who was daydreaming or absent-minded; one sixteenth-century writer notes 'As though our wittes and our senses were a woll gathering', an allusion, perhaps, to a wool-gatherer's endless, low-reward wandering.

For some women and girls, especially those who fell between the cracks of 'normal' households - such as orphans, widows, the elderly and unmarried women - knitting wool would have been one of the only legitimate ways of earning an income, albeit a modest one. It was also seen as an appropriate and potentially profitable skill for female inmates of workhouses and orphanages. York, for example, had a 'knitting school' as early as 1614 in St Anthony's, a medieval guildhall, with the express aim of teaching knitting to the city's poor children. It's perhaps telling that the building was also, intermittently, a workhouse and a 'house of correction'. Workhouses expected their inhabitants to knit - especially women and girls - to help pay for their keep and, hopefully, learn a trade. Failure to toe the line was dealt with swiftly and harshly - one entry from an English workhouse in Berkshire, from 1852, shows the punishment handed out to Mary Bowler, an agricultural labourer in her mid-twenties who had been in and out of the workhouse, and trouble, since the age of fifteen:

Mary Bowler, a young woman and an inmate of the Farringdon Union, was on the 5th inst., brought before the Rev. J. F. Cleaver and Sir R. G. Throckmorton, charged by the Governor with having refused to perform the work assigned her, namely, knitting socks; she was committed to Reading Gaol for 21 days' hard labour.[3]

Religious schools also expected their pupils to learn handicrafts, especially wool knitting, partly as a life skill but often as a way of making a contribution to the school's finances by creating items – such as stockings – that could be sold. Ackworth School, founded in 1779 near Pontefract in Yorkshire, was a Quaker school for children whose parents were 'not in affluence'. Alongside religious lessons and the three Rs, children – both girls and boys – were encouraged to knit, spin and do needlework to boost the school's bank balance. In 1821, records show that the female students knitted 339 stockings.[4] Far from being seen as exploitative, such work was regarded by many people in Georgian and Victorian society as a necessary way for the poor – including children – to earn their keep, lest they fall back into their 'idle' ways. Indeed, when Ackworth School turned away from menial work to focus on more progressive academic training, not everyone who knew the school was thrilled. In a letter written to *The British Friend* – a Quaker magazine – dated 1847, one irate reader complains that Ackworth School seems to have lost its way:

Great stress appears now, however to be laid upon mental training. Formerly, industrial training was in high repute; and of the two, the latter perhaps of the greater importance to the children of the middling, and poorer class of society. Industrial Schools were far more common in England, during and prior to the last century, than they are now, particularly in the city of Norwich; where the children, from 6 to 10 years of age, earned several thousand pounds a-year more than supplied them with food and clothing, merely by knitting fine Jersey stockings [...] Spinning and knitting were very generally taught in schools formerly, and practised to great advantage. If Ackworth was turned more into an industrial school, it might have the effect of thinning the number in the school at one time; and thus have rendered the proposed extension of the premises unnecessary.[5]

Before 1880, when elementary education became compulsory up to the age of ten in Britain, working-class education was often piecemeal, poorly regulated and, in the case of girls, focused around textiles, especially wool. Unregulated schools – such as dame schools or charity schools – were often 'overcrowded, ill ventilated, heated by a single stove, almost totally unequipped; and their educational value was further reduced by the mistress' frequently leaving the room to tend the shop she also kept or to quiet her babies'.[6]

In 1832 the Church of England released a book entitled *The National Society's Instructions on Needlework and Knitting*, which was designed to teach children 'suitable work for the lower classes', including knitting wool stockings. As late as the First World War, guides were being released to teach very young working-class children remarkably complex knitting patterns – Ethel M. Dudley's *Knitting for Infants and Juniors*, published in 1914, insisted, with great enthusiasm, that 'practical use can be accomplished by tiny fingers'.

Even if girls were lucky enough to go to school, it didn't lessen the burden of chores they had to carry out at home. Hannah Mitchell, a suffragette and social activist born in 1871, remembers her experiences bitterly:

On winter evenings there was sewing by hand, making and mending shirts and underwear. At eight years old my weekly task was to darn all the stockings for the household, and I think my first reactions to feminism began at this time when I was forced to darn my brothers' stockings while they read or played cards or dominoes. Sometimes the boys helped with rugmaking, or in cutting up wool or picking feathers for beds and pillows, but for them this was voluntary work; for the girls it was compulsory, and the fact that the boys could read if they wished, filled my cup with bitterness to the brim.[7]

Knitting wasn't only seen as a suitable pastime for poor women and girls. Over the course of the nineteenth century, it gradually came to be regarded as a craft with potential for respectable, well-to-do ladies. The girls of rich families were expected to acquire a suite of suitable skills in preparation for marriage – embroidery, singing, playing the piano, dancing and other 'feminine' pursuits were encouraged, alongside knitting. For many bright and creative but woefully under-stimulated middle- and upper-class women, knitting represented a chance to do something useful; a way of creating small items to sell for a good cause or making decorative pieces such as pincushions and egg cosies for around the home.

Even Queen Victoria was never too far from a pair of knitting needles, famously running up mittens and scarves for British soldiers fighting in the Crimean War. For Victoria, spinning and knitting wool were clearly treasured outlets for both artistic expression and energy – there are accounts of her knitting while being read to by her beloved governess, knitting while convalescing in bed, and knitting beautiful quilts and cot covers for her children and grandchildren. There's a fabulous photograph in the Royal Collection of an elderly Queen Victoria – dressed from head to toe in black, of course – comfortably nestled in a large armchair, listening to her youngest daughter Beatrice read the newspaper aloud; the queen is listening intently, knitting needles in hand and ball of wool unwinding at her feet. It's an unusually intimate portrait of Victoria, captured, on the face of it, in a rare moment of quiet relaxation. For anyone who saw the photograph, the symbolism of the wool could not have been clearer: if knitting was a craft embraced by the 'Great Mother' of the nation, it was surely an eminently respectable way for any lady of quality to spend her time – and to 'do her bit'.

While the daily lives of wealthy women would have been markedly different from those of their working-class sisters, both shared similar limitations on their scope for playing a role in public or political activities. Knitting, and other needle arts, became an important way for women to express themselves, sometimes in subversive ways. Before the American Revolutionary War (1775–83), the United States had a strong tradition of hand knitting, brought over by settlers predominantly from Britain. In one instance, in the late 1630s, twenty families from the village of Rowley in East Yorkshire emigrated to Massachusetts, taking their wool-working skills with them and founding the settlement of Rowley in Essex County, which they intended to establish as a new centre for weaving and clothmaking. When they got there, the men of Rowley built a fulling mill to process the cloth, while the women got on with processing the raw wool for their husbands' craft and furiously hand knitting at home.[8]

The ability to knit was seen not only as a necessary life skill for women, but as a symbol of self-sufficiency and a can-do pioneering spirit. Making woollen clothes, blankets and other items for the home became both the hallmark of the 'ideal' frontier wife but also the means by which individuals could, by showing that they could cope without foreign woollen imports, sever old colonial ties.

During the seventeenth century British woollen merchants made vast profits, selling their cloth both at home and around the world. The new colonists of America, however, didn't want to buy English cloth; they wanted to make their own. Britain had been keeping a close eye on the American settlers almost from the word go; just a few years after the Pilgrim Fathers had landed, early settlers had bought forty sheep from Dutch traders. These, and others that were subsequently purchased from the Spanish, and more imported by the London Company, allowed the settlers just enough to start breeding sheep, making their own cloth and producing a surplus of wool that could be traded. Britain was furious at this blatant attempt at economic self-sufficiency and threatened serious punishments for anyone caught exporting sheep to the colonies. As Adam Smith noted in his *Wealth of Nations*:

... the exporter of sheep, lambs or rams, was for the first offence to forfeit all his goods for ever, to suffer a year's imprisonment, and then to have his left hand cut off in a market town upon a market day, to be there nailed up; and for second offence to be adjudged a felon, and to suffer death accordingly.[9]

A similar fate was promised for anyone in the colonies caught trading in wool. The settlers were defiant, however, and not only managed to quickly build a cottage cloth industry but also had the audacity, in British eyes, to start trading with one another, and with other European countries. Wool production became so important that by 1662 Virginia was offering five pounds of tobacco (the unit of currency at the time) for every yard of wool cloth made in its own colony,[10] and by 1664 Massachusetts had brought in a law that required children to learn how to spin and weave wool.[11] Supply could barely keep up with demand – one academic has estimated that every adult in a household would need thirty to forty yards of wool just to have enough for basic clothing; with 30,000 adults living in New England by 1665, this equates to roughly 1.2 million yards (1,098,000 metres) of wool fabric.[12]

All this wool-related economic activity provoked the fury of the king of England. In 1699 William III issued *An Act to prevent the Exportation of Wool out of the Kingdoms of Ireland and England into Forreigne parts and for the Incouragement of the Woollen Manufactures in the Kingdom of England.* It was designed with three express aims – first, to force the colonies to only import British wool; second, to ban colonists from exporting wool out of America; and third, to tax any sales of wool.

The wearing of homespun wool cloth by the colonists – which was often a blend of wool and linen called *linsey woolsey* or *wincey* – became a mark of defiance and symbol of patriotism. Families, communities and church groups would hold 'spinning bees' to see who could make the most woollen yarn, often taking the opportunity to discuss political issues of the day. Women – by creating and buying homespun textiles, and boycotting British ones – were seen as key figures of civil disobedience in the colonial resistance. When the college that would later become Brown University was first founded in Providence, Rhode Island, in the 1760s, the president deliberately wore homespun clothing during the inaugural ceremony; over at Harvard, in Massachusetts, both teaching staff and scholars also wore homespun clothing in solidarity.[13] And, while there were many subsequent efforts by Britain to control and stifle American trade – such as the Sugar Act of 1764 and the Tea Act of 1773 – it was the Wool Act of 1699 that sewed the first stitches of rebellion and anger in the colonies that led, ultimately, to America's Revolutionary War between 1775 and 1783 and its Declaration of Independence.

By the time of the Revolutionary War, colonial women were so used to clothing their families in homespun fabrics and hand-knitted garments that it came as no surprise when they were asked to provide clothing and blankets for the soldiers who were going into battle on their behalf. A clothier-general was appointed to assess the army's requirements for bedding and uniform – vast quantities of knitters were needed if the army was going to keep its men warm.

Towns published the names and knitting tallies of their inhabitants, to encourage a spirit of competition, and women from all walks of life - including George Washington's wife Martha, who became the inaugural First Lady of the United States - were encouraged to add their contribution, however small. Desperate reports from the front line of soldiers poorly dressed and fighting in bare feet kept knitters at their needles, often recycling old textiles into new stockings, blankets and breeches for 'the boys'.

The plight of American soldiers, and women's efforts to clothe them, was also later immortalized in Louisa May Alcott's *Little Women* (1880), set during the Civil War in the early 1860s: 'Beth said nothing, but wiped away her tears with the blue army sock and began to knit with all her might, losing no time in doing the duty that lay nearest her, while she resolved in her quiet little soul to be all that Father hoped to find her when the year brought round the happy coming home.' Our heroine Jo, however, finds the task of knitting socks for the war - and its gendered undertones - a little more irksome:

'It's bad enough to be a girl, anyway, when I like boy's games and work and manners! I can't get over my disappointment in not being a boy. And it's worse than ever now, for I'm dying to go and fight with Papa. And I can only stay home and knit, like a poky old woman!' And

Jo shook the blue army sock till the needles rattled like castanets, and her ball bounded across the room.

Knitting also has a rich and fascinating heritage as an innocent front for covert deeds and spying. Again, in the American Revolutionary War, as the British occupied Philadelphia, legend tells of one tavern owner – Molly 'Old Mom' Rinker – who would listen in on enemy soldiers whose tongues had been loosened by alcohol. Conversations she'd overhear in her pub during the evening, about troop movements or enemy strategy, would be quickly scribbled down and then tucked into balls of wool. During the day, she'd walk to her favourite rocky mound and sit and knit socks, while surreptitiously lowering her message-laden balls of wool over the edge of the cliff behind her and into the hands of a colonial dispatch rider.

Knitting was also the perfect vehicle for coded messages – by making a specific pattern, messages could be hidden in an innocent run of stitches or a custom-made piece of clothing. During both world wars the Belgian Resistance enlisted old women to live in houses with views of railway stations or lines. As vehicles and trains came and went, the women would add different stitches into their knitting – knit one for a train, purl one for an artillery vehicle, and so on, which could then be handed on to fellow spies. Wool yarn suited Morse code-style messages perfectly, with different knots being 'read' as either dots or dashes. Far from being a twee idea, the authorities treated it with deadly seriousness; during the Second World War, for example, America's Office of Censorship banned knitting patterns being posted abroad, just in case they might contain sensitive, coded information.

But often just the act of knitting was enough of a disguise. No one suspected women, gently working away with their wool, were using the activity as a cover for espionage. One American, Elizabeth Bentley, who initially spied for the Soviets during the Second World War before defecting and becoming an informer for the FBI, famously used her knitting bag to conceal classified information and aircraft plans that she'd stolen. Another who used knitting as a cover for sending secret messages was the Frenchwoman Madame Levengle. During the First World War she would watch German troop movements from her bedroom window, while knitting and tapping her foot on the floor. Meanwhile, her children downstairs – who were busy pretending to do homework – would jot down the sequence of taps, all under the nose of a German guard posted in their home.[14] The British had their own knitting spy too. In 1944, at only twenty-three years of age, secret agent Phyllis Latour Doyle was parachuted into Nazi-occupied Normandy to gather intelligence for the forthcoming D-Day landings. In just a few short months, posing as a poor fourteen-year-old French girl, Doyle relayed 135 coded messages which she would hide in her knitting, before passing them onto the British military. For all its *'Allo 'Allo* charm to modern eyes, the mission was hugely risky. Talking to a magazine journalist later in life, Doyle recalled: 'The men who had been sent just before me were caught and executed. I was told I was chosen for that area [of France] because I would arouse less suspicion.'[15]

While many examples of knitting codes come from the era of the two world wars, it wasn't a new idea. In 1859 Dickens famously created the character of Madame Defarge in *A Tale of Two Cities*, who takes great pleasure from knitting while she watches the guillotine slice its way through the French nobility. As she sits and coolly sees heads roll, she knits the names of the victims into her knitting, as a kind of roll-call of revenge. Her character was based on real-life *tricoteuses* – working-class women who would take their knitting to public executions and fastidiously clack away while watching the spectacle unfold. Denied access to any form of legitimate assembly, the *tricoteuses* gathered instead as spectators, all the while knitting, among other things, 'liberty caps' for the revolutionaries.

While most *tricoteuses* were probably just sullen observers, fictional accounts often treated them as bloodthirsty voyeurs. Baroness Orczy's novel *The Scarlet Pimpernel* (1908) paints the picture with grisly glee:

The women who drove the carts usually spent their day on the Place de la Greve, beneath the platform of the guillotine, knitting and gossiping, whilst they watched the rows of tumbrils arriving with the victims the Reign of Terror claimed every day. It was great fun to see the aristos arriving for the reception of Madame la Guillotine, and the places close by the platform were very much sought after. Bibot, during the day, had been on duty on the Place. He recognized most of the old hags, 'tricotteuses,' as they were called, who sat there and knitted whilst head after head fell beneath the knife, and they themselves got quite bespattered with the blood of those cursed aristos.

But perhaps the most famous examples of wool and war work, however, are the 'Knit for Victory' campaigns. During the First World War, knitting fever swept across Britain. Soldiers' letters, describing appalling trench conditions and freezing temperatures, spurred women, children and men who were unable to serve to start making and sending items of knitwear in their millions. Socks, gloves, mittens, balaclavas, vests, blankets and sweaters were fashioned in vast numbers by loved ones desperate to raise morale on the front and feel part of the war effort. Magazines, posters and knitting patterns of the day urged eager knitters to 'Knit a Bit' for the war effort and show 'Our Boys' they were not forgotten.

Guides were issued to show knitters how to create essential bits of kit – the *British Journal of Nursing* offered guidance on mufflers, *The Graphic* newspaper showed how old socks and stockings could be repurposed as mittens, and *The Queen* magazine published how-to guides on knitting for needy soldiers, including instructions for how to make rifle gloves, balaclavas with ear flaps and knitted leg warmers. Other patterns were copied from women's magazines, such as *Woman's Own*, or charity booklets designed specifically to help clothe servicemen abroad.

Even wool companies got in on the act: the British firm Weldon's printed dozens of designs, many of them remarkably specialized for the amateur knitter. In their pamphlet *Garments and Hospital Comforts for our Soldiers and Sailors*, women at home were encouraged to create a raft of military and therapeutic garments, including woollen helmets with ear openings, stockings, abdominal belts, heelless day socks, convertible scarves, knitted finger stalls, bed socks, sea-boot stockings for sailors, and even knitted eye bandages. The pamphlet also suggested that ladies tuck notes into their knitted presents, with messages of support such as 'God protect you', 'Everyone is thinking of you' and 'Good luck to you brave men'.

Some of the soldiers who received their woollen gifts felt compelled to write back, thanking the knitter for their efforts. Archives from St John's, Newfoundland, include a note written by Edward Noftall, age nineteen, to a Miss Clarke of Twillingate in the summer of 1918:

Dear Miss CLARKE: – Just a note thanking you for the socks which were very nice indeed and in such a place as France. I know the people in Twillingate must work hard working for the soldiers of Nfld. I don't know if I know any of your friends out here, but I can tell you that all the boys that are here at present are feeling well. My address is 83 E.G. NOFTALL, 1st Royal Nfld. Regt. B.E.F., France.

Your friend, Ted.[16]

In their letters home, some soldiers made promises to visit the women who had knitted their socks; for a lucky few, it was the beginning of a new friendship or love affair. Not for poor Edward, however. Only a few months after writing his thank-you note to Miss Clarke, and just weeks before the end of the war, Edward died from appendicitis, in a Belgian hospital some 2,500 miles (4,000 kilometres) from home.

Not all woolly contributions were as well received as others, however; knitting skills back home varied enormously, as did the quality of the yarn. Magazines such as *Tatler* featured humorous cartoons poking gentle fun at rogue knitters and their efforts, while one New Zealand soldier's poem of the time reads:

Life of a pair of socks
They are some fit!
I used one for a helmet

And the other for a mitt
Glad to hear
You're doing your bit
But who the...
Said you could knit?[17]

When the United States joined the Allied effort in April 1917, knitting became a patriotic duty there too. The US government quickly set to work securing essential equipment for the soldiers; and while they managed to scrape together the basics needed for survival, including heavy overcoats, American soldiers were woefully undersupplied with warm garments such as hats, gloves and jumpers.

The American Red Cross sprang into action, handing out woollen yarn and knitting patterns, demanding that everyone – from prisoners to pensioners – 'Knit for Sammy'. Even President Wilson and his wife Edith got involved by allowing sheep to graze the grass in front of the White House and then auctioning off the wool, raising thousands of dollars for the American Red Cross. The campaign to mobilize American knitters paid off – in just a year and half, US citizens knitted over 24 million items of clothing for soldiers.[18]

People click-clacked away at home, at work, on public transport and even at play. In California, female lifeguards knitted on the beach; in Seattle, a jury knitted as they mulled over a verdict; the New York Philharmonic Society was even forced to issue a plea to audience members to stop disrupting performances with their incessant knitting. Men got in on the act too – firemen knitted through their watch, train conductors between stations; injured soldiers in their recovery wards knitted; even the inmates of America's prisons did their bit with needle and wool.[19]

Over in Australia, civilian groups also knitted throughout the Great War, coordinated through organizations such as the Comforts Fund and the Soldiers' Sock Fund, who also provided instructional talks to steer knitters in the right direction. Over 1.3 million socks were sent overseas from Australia. Demand often outstripped supply – not only did knitters have to keep up a furious pace to keep up with soldiers' needs, but there simply weren't enough needles to go round. Ever resourceful, the inhabitants of the state of Victoria turned bicycle spokes into knitting needles and even sold on those converted spokes that they did not need to other states.

Wool was also in fierce demand. Before the First World War, Australia had an almost complete monopoly of world wool production; with the outbreak of war, the UK government asked Australia to stop exporting its wool to anywhere except Britain, leading to a steep drop in wool prices. Only after lengthy negotiations in 1916 did the British government agree to buy Australia's entire wool production for the rest of the war at a fairer rate – 55 per cent more than the pre-war price. The country's wool industry recovered but, with wool in short supply, Australia needed to find an alternative. Soon a scheme was in place to send sheepskin vests for every Australian soldier posted abroad. By the end of the year, 150,000 sheepskin vests - stitched together by volunteers - were warming the backs of Australian boys fighting in the trenches of the Western Front.

The huge effort that wool knitters put into military clothing and blankets paid off. Not only did the free labour of volunteers supplement those domestic textile industries struggling to keep pace with demand, but the health benefits of warm woollen clothes helped Allied soldiers tough out, and ultimately win, a war in which cold and wet were as deadly an enemy as the German army. The knitting campaign also had an emotional impact on soldiers, reminding them of support back home, and on the knitters left behind who wanted desperately to connect and help. Knitted clothes represented a physical link to home, family and the loving embrace of a sweetheart. Mothers, daughters, fathers and other family members knitted garments in the knowledge that these might be the last clothes a young soldier ever wore - and that they might 'end with him, bloodstained and far from home.'[20]

Who could have guessed that only a few years later, many of the same people who had knitted for victory in the First World War would be called on to do the same again in a second global conflict. As *Time* magazine announced in 1940, 'The men hardly have time to grab their guns before their wives and sweethearts grab their needles and yarn.'[21] For them, knitting was a familiar and immediate reaction to war despite the fact that, by this time, machine knitting was much more efficient. Alongside claims from knitters that hand-crafted textiles were more robust than factory ones, and that hand knitting didn't use up precious fuel or machinery, civilians knitted for victory because, for their own sanity, they *had* to. In the words of an article printed in *The New York Times* in January 1942:

> The propaganda effect of hand knitting cannot be estimated in terms of hard cash, but it is considerable. A sweater for a bluejacket. A helmet for a flying cadet, made by some devoted woman in a small town far from the war, is sure to arouse interest in the navy or Air Force among the friends of the woman doing the knitting. And she herself feels that she has an active part in this vast conflict; she is not useless, although she can do nothing else to help win the war.[22]

10

'SHEEPE HATH PAYED FOR IT ALL'

Wool churches, white monks and the crime of owling

I n the space of just one year, between 1338 and 1339, William
de la Pole – a wool merchant from Hull – lent King Edward III
an eye-watering amount of cash; around £118,000 or, in today's
money, the best part of £167 million.[1] And he could well afford
to. By the time of his death, in 1366, William was one of the
richest men in England and had established the de la Pole
family name as one of the great aristocratic houses.

His son, Michael, became Earl of Suffolk and only a century
later his descendant got within a whisker of the throne when
Richard III named John de la Pole as his heir. Had the outcome
of the Battle of Bosworth of 1485 been different, and Henry
Tudor lost, the direct descendant of a fleece dealer would have
become king of England. The meteoric rise of this spectacularly
successful entrepreneur, from keen-eyed trader to nobility in
one generation, reflects a moment in England's history when
wool made the country very, *very* wealthy indeed.

By the time William de la Pole was born, the English
wool business had been trundling along for centuries. After
the Romans landed on English shores in AD 43, they soon

established a well-organized wool industry. The country already had its native, small Soay-like horned sheep that had wandered the Isles since the Bronze Age, but we know from historical records that by AD 300 the wool that was coming out of Britain was, according to the geographer Dionysius Periegetes, 'so fine that it was comparable to a spider's web'.[2]

One idea is that the Romans brought their own flocks over from the Mediterranean – fine, white-woolled sheep that preferred the rich grasslands, marshes and fens of the south and southeast of England, regions that were to become the great wool-producing areas such as Suffolk, Norfolk and the Cotswolds.

It's difficult to know what the English sheep and wool 'industry' looked like after the Romans finally abandoned Britain in AD 410 and in the years we erroneously call the 'Dark Ages'; we just don't have many sources to draw on. But the few documents that do exist suggest plenty of people were keeping sheep, especially for wool. One of the earliest records in 697 shows King Wihtred of Kent granting pastureland for 300 sheep in 'Rumining seta' (now Romney Marsh) to St Mary's Church, Lyminge.[3]

In 796 Charlemagne, king of the Franks, wrote to Offa, king of Mercia in Anglo-Saxon England – the letter is the oldest surviving diplomatic document in English history and mentions, among other things, the woollen cloaks the Mercians were trading with the Franks. The letter hints at an older trading arrangement in woollen cloth; Charlemagne mentions that his subjects would dearly like to buy cloaks of the same style 'as they used to come us in old times'.[4] And, as we saw in Chapter Five, the fact that we have hundreds of ovine place names that begin with Ship, Shap, Shep or Skip, relics of Anglo-Saxon and Norse words for sheep, suggests an early medieval world of lively sheep farming and trading both within, and out of, the British Isles.

By the time of the Domesday Book in 1086, sheep were the number one agricultural commodity – one survey taken soon after the Norman Conquest showed there were more sheep across England than all the cows, pigs and poultry put together. Between them, the large estates in Norfolk, Suffolk, Essex, Cambridgeshire, Cornwall, Devon, Somerset and Dorset had nearly 300,000 sheep. The monks at Ely Abbey, in Cambridgeshire, had more than 13,000 alone.

Many of the large-scale owners of sheep were monasteries or religious orders – records from the beginning of the twelfth century, for example, show a group of nuns keeping nearly two thousand sheep grazing on Minchinhampton Common in the Cotswolds.[5] When Richard I managed to get himself captured by Duke Leopold of Austria on his return from a crusade at the end of the twelfth century, his 150,000 marks ransom (about £200 million in today's money) was paid for, in part, by 50,000 sacks of English wool, pretty much the entire wool clip from the English Cistercian and

Premonstratensian houses; textile historians have worked out that this colossal amount of wool would have needed between 10 and 13 million sheep[6] - that's about four sheep for every man, woman and child across England, Wales and Scotland combined.[7] (The rest of Richard's ransom money was scraped together by other measures, including a universal tax of 25 per cent on all incomes, from earls and barons to merchants and yeomen, and 'donations' of gold and silver vessels from churches.)

Monasteries were particularly well placed to rear sheep for wool - many of them owned or had been gifted vast, open tracts of pastureland, much of it suitable only for sheep grazing. They also had ample labour available in the form of *conversi* (waged farming monks) and lay workers from surrounding villages. Monasteries acted as 'central depots' for fleeces from outlaying farms and granges, a collection point where the entire region's wool clip could be dumped, graded and bundled ready for export.

The Cistercians also cornered the market in preparing wool, cannily adding value by meticulously washing, drying, sorting, weighing and carefully packaging it, a process that was often too time-consuming and costly for small-scale farmers.[8] Interestingly, the Cistercians became known as the 'White Monks'. It was traditional for monks to wear dark habits, but the Cistercians decided that they would shun the use of expensive dyes and, instead, wear undyed, off-white woollen clothing to proclaim their poverty. For some, the gesture smacked of superiority over the more 'ostentatious' orders such as the Benedictines. For others, the wearing of white, woollen habits perfectly expressed the Cistercians' moral purity. As the Cistercian monk and writer Walter Daniel wrote in the late twelfth century:

> For their name arose from the fact that, as the angels might be, they were clothed in undyed wool, spun and woven from the pure fleece of sheep. So named and garbed and gathered together like flocks of seagulls they shine as they walk with the whiteness of snow.[9]

One of the great ironies of the wool trade is that the monasteries, who started sheep farming as a means of living an austere, self-sufficient life, became really rather good at it. Many of the religious houses across the country became so adept at the 'business of wool' they started to sell futures in their own products. Wool traders would agree to buy three or four years' worth of wool in advance; they sometimes even acquired a wool clip as much as twenty years before the sheep were actually shorn. The monasteries liked this arrangement as it provided them with a means of financial planning – wool prices could fluctuate wildly from one year to the next. It also gave them a ready source of cash for running costs, papal taxes and building works. Wool merchants liked the arrangement because it gave them guaranteed – and often heavily discounted – access to a competitive, highly prized product.

Most of the agreements for the advance sale of wool were made between Italian merchants and monastic orders in England. By effectively lending the monasteries money, the Italian merchants made vast profits from two sources – one from the sale of the finished cloth (or selling the wool to other Italian cloth manufacturers) but also by charging high interest on the loans made against the wool, typically between 10 and 40 per cent.[10]

A handful of Italian families dominated the highly lucrative dual businesses of wool trading and banking; the most famous of all, the Medici family, controlled political, social and cultural life in Florence for the best part of three hundred years, from the fourteenth to the seventeenth century. The Medici, with their head for business and appetite for shrewd alliances, went from small-scale wool producers to global bankers and a political dynasty in just a few generations. Wealth bought power, but it also paid for the patronage of some of the greatest artists and thinkers of the Renaissance; without the wool-trading, money-lending Medici family, we may have never had some of the greatest artistic, scientific and architectural achievements of all time. The House of Medici supported, among many others, Brunelleschi, Donatello, Fra Angelico, Botticelli, Leonardo da Vinci, Machiavelli, Michelangelo and Galileo, bankrolled the invention of the piano, and funded the development of opera as an art form. As well as marrying into various European royal families, the Medicis also produced four popes; one, in particular, was the hardliner Pope Clement VII (1523-34) whose claim to fame was his excommunication of Henry VIII of England from the Catholic Church for annulling his marriage to Catherine of Aragon and marrying Anne Boleyn.

Back in the monasteries, the heady combination of wool farming and big bank loans didn't always go to plan. Easy credit almost always comes with a crash. Even in good times, historical documents suggest that about one in ten advance contracts fell through, when monasteries couldn't deliver on their promises. During spells of widespread sheep disease the numbers of disappointed buyers must have been considerably higher. The debt records for Rievaulx Abbey in Yorkshire, for example, reveal a spectacular fall from grace. Throughout the 1280s, the abbey had been playing two wealthy Italian merchants off each other, promising advance wool clips to both parties for huge sums of money. The abbey had large running costs and an ambitious building programme to fund, so 'mortgaging' their future wool crop seemed a smart move. Instead, the sheep flock was devastated by scab, leaving Rievaulx with a growing mountain of debt. By 1291, with costs spiralling, the abbot was humiliatingly forced to disperse the congregation, close its doors to guests and travellers, and send his monks off to different Cistercian houses in the area until the abbey's cashflow improved.[11]

By the fourteenth century most English-grown fleeces were being shipped abroad to two destinations in particular – the Low Countries and Florence, both of which were centres of excellence when it came to fine cloth. But, because there just wasn't enough local wool to meet demand and the home-grown fleeces available were far too coarse to weave into their 'incomparable cloth', both places were forced to import wool in huge quantities. England's wool-exporting was greatly facilitated by its French territorial possessions – the region of Gascony, in the southwest, and, crucially, the Channel port of Calais, in the northeast.

Some imports of fine wool came from Burgundy and Spain – the Berbers, from North Africa, had introduced the Merino breed, with its white, curly fleece, to southern Spain in the 1100s – but it was Britain, with its predecessors of modern fine wool breeds such as the Cotswold and the Lincoln, who stole the lead. For once, Britain's rainy climate had given her the edge, the wet weather ensuring a longer grazing season and plenty of lush grass for wool sheep to thrive.

England's hold over the wool market was well known, even at the time – one thirteenth-century poet from Artois used the phrase 'carrying wool to England' in the same way we would now say 'carry coals to Newcastle'.[12] If export supplies were interrupted, foreign weavers soon suffered: 'In 1297, when such a stoppage took place, the land of Flanders', claimed the English chronicler Heminburgh, was 'well nigh empty [...]

because the people cannot have the wools of England.'[13] Only forty years later, in 1337, when Edward III temporarily stopped all exports of wool to much of Europe, the Low Countries were, again, quickly brought to their knees.

The prosperity of the nation depended so heavily on wool that 'The barons of England, sitting in Parliament, asserted... that wool represented half of England's wealth.'[14] Edward III knew this only too well – when he needed money to underwrite his military ambitions against France it was the wool industry he turned to. His objectives were twofold: firstly, to raise as much cash as he could by taxing the most profitable trade in England, and, second, to use wool exports as a weapon to 'persuade' his allies to join him. By threatening to stop English wool from entering those foreign regions who relied on it – such as Flanders – Edward III could bully his diplomatic 'friends' into allegiance.

In one year alone, English wool merchants loaned Edward III over £250 million in today's money and pledged to pay him half the profit on 30,000 sacks of wool. In return, only those merchants who agreed to the deal would be allowed to export wool aboard. Indeed, so obsessed was Edward III with the wool trade that he ordered his Lord Chancellor to sit on a bale of wool during council, to symbolize the importance of wool to the English economy.

The 'Woolsack' is the name now given to the wool-stuffed seat occupied by the Lord Speaker in the House of Lords, a huge square cushion covered in crimson cloth. In 1938, when the woolsack came to be reupholstered, it was discovered, rather embarrassingly, that over the centuries, its wool contents had been bolstered with cheaper, coarser horsehair. Needless to say, it was hastily re-stuffed with wool from around Britain and the Commonwealth as a symbol of unity. And, while the original Woolsack is well-known as a Parliamentary symbol, there is actually *another* one. Just behind the Woolsack is the Judges' Woolsack – an even larger cushion occupied by senior judges during State Openings (and by members of the Lords during normal sittings of the House) and a throwback to the days when legal advisers played a key role in medieval parliaments.

Between the thirteenth and fifteenth centuries wool made certain members of medieval English society very rich. As Joseph Hall, bishop of Norwich, declared in the seventeenth century: 'There were wont to be reckoned three wonders of England, *ecclesia*, *foemina*, *lana* – churches, women and wool.' Ports such as London, Southampton, Boston and Hull expanded to cope with the ever-increasing volume of wool exports – duties were collected at each major port by specially appointed tax men called 'collectors', who would then pass on the money to 'customers' who ensured that it made its way safely back to the City of London and into the pockets of the Exchequer.

'Searchers' were also employed at the ports, to make sure all the correct duties had been paid, and to arrest anyone dealing in counterfeit cash. Wool merchants were asked to present themselves at specially arranged 'custom houses'; there, a huge set of scales weighed the packages of wool destined for abroad and the duty was calculated on the spot. During the busiest times, almost 98 per cent of customs revenue came from wool exports alone. And, although the first written evidence for levying customs duties dates back to the age of King Aethelbald of Mercia in the eighth century, we have sheep to thank for establishing Her Majesty's Customs on a basis still recognizable today.

Not everyone was willing to pay export taxes, however. 'Owling' – so called because it was usually carried out at night, and smugglers would 'hoot' signals to each other – was the crime of smuggling sheep or wool out of the country. The punishments for those who were caught owling, which were enshrined in law by Edward III, were particularly brutal. Statutes from the time of Elizabeth I demand that anyone apprehended 'shall suffer imprisonment by the space of one whole yere [...] and at the yeres ende shall in soome open Market Towne in the fulnesse of the Market on the Market Daye have his lefte hande cut of and that to be nayled up in the openest place of suche Market.'[15] Other later amendments to the law included the added humiliations of confiscation of goods, three years' imprisonment for the master and all the mariners of the offending vessel, and transportation to the colonies for seven years.

During the seventeenth century owling was rife, especially on the vast open stretches of Romney Marsh in southeast England. On a clear day, smugglers could see France from the shoreline of Kent and East Sussex; many of them were also local fishermen, who knew the coastal caves and creeks of the Channel well, making it possible for them to load ships in secret and sail under cover of darkness. In 1689, a bill was passed that outlawed all trade with France, in the hope of protecting Britain's woollen textile industry; but it only served to redouble owlers' efforts – in the same year 480,000 pounds (218,000 kg) of wool were smuggled to France.[16]

Far from being a romantic, Robin Hood-esque enterprise, smuggling on England's south coast had become an organized criminal activity, catering to a wide and greedy market. From the last gasps of the 1600s to the first breaths of the 1800s, smuggling was a pitiless business, often 'violent, ruthless and bloody in the extreme, even when judged by the brutal standards of the time'.[17] Almost everyone, it seems, was in on it. Criminal gangs were often financed by local gentry, pro-tected by bent magistrates, and hidden by local villagers and townsfolk. Even revenue officers weren't above taking bribes. Only the occasional brave soul felt able to take matters into their own hands: in 1714, Hugh Harsnet, a customs official, and Daniel Gates, a mariner, took it upon themselves to prosecute an owler, one Thomas Tanner, for illegally exporting wool. Amazingly, they won. And bagged a forty-shilling reward in the process,[18] the equivalent of about twenty-two days' wages for a skilled tradesman.

For Harsnet and Gates, the reward would have been a welcome windfall, but it was small fry compared to the staggering amounts of money made by the savviest wool merchants during the height of the wool trade. One of the earliest and most successful entrepreneurs was Laurence of Ludlow, a rich tradesman for whom wool bought property, influence and the ear of the king. From the 1270s, Laurence was an enthusiastic wool trader, a business he inherited from his late father. He dealt in fleeces from local monasteries, farmers and landed gentry around Shropshire and the Welsh Marches and, when he wasn't working at one of his offices in either Shrewsbury or London, Laurence would go on business trips abroad – to the great trade fairs of Champagne, for instance – to strike lucrative wool deals.

With his money Laurence bought the manor of Stokesay and began building his dream home – Stokesay Castle – now one of the best-preserved medieval manor houses in England. Wealth also bought him influence in court; when Edward I threatened to seize the entire country's wool supply, Laurence persuaded him to raise funds by hiking up the custom rate on wool exports instead. Laurence also became the king's paymaster, delivering both wool and money to his allies overseas.

On one of these trips, however, disaster struck. In November

1294, Laurence's fleet left for Flanders. After only a few days at sea, the ships ran into a storm and Laurence's vessel was wrecked off the Suffolk coast. News of Laurence's death travelled fast; wool producers, who had been hit hard by Edward I's draconian tax, could barely conceal their delight. As one chronicler - the annalist of Dunstable Abbey wrote, because Laurence 'sinned against the wool-growers, he was swallowed by the waves in a ship full of wool.'[19] Medieval businessmen clearly weren't a sentimental lot - only days after his drowning, some of Laurence's wool was recovered from the sea, dried off and resold for a tidy profit.[20]

Not every wool merchant met a sticky end, of course. Many of the farmers, middlemen and landowners made rich by the medieval wool trade went on to build some of the country's finest houses, guildhalls and public buildings. And some of England's prettiest, most chocolate-box towns and villages - places such as Hadleigh, Lavenham, Long Melford, Bury St Edmunds and Clare in Suffolk, and Chipping Camden, Burford, Stow-on-the-Wold and Bibury in Gloucestershire - owe their embarrassment of architectural riches to the wool trade.

Lavish spending wasn't just confined to domestic buildings. Families who had grown wealthy on wool made vast contributions to the construction or enlargement of their local parish churches, often creating places of worship that were completely out of scale with the tiny village congregation. Their motives were mixed - a heady cocktail of genuine piety, the desire to show off and bleak cynicism encouraged wealthy donors. Visible acts of charity or 'indulgences' were the quickest, if not the cheapest, way for a well-to-do merchant and his family to smooth their path to heaven.

The 'Cathedral of the Cotswolds', St Peter and St Paul, in Northleach, for example, is a formidable memorial to the local wool merchants whose lives were transformed by wool. The church was not only rebuilt and refurbished with wool money in the mid-fifteenth century – when Northleach was the most prosperous and important wool town in the Cotswolds – but also contains many medieval 'brasses', memorial plaques to local benefactors. Most of the merchants shown on the plaques have their feet resting on or near sheep and woolpacks, to show the origins of their fortune.

There are fascinating clues to the wool trade hidden within the brasses – on one, a woman has her foot on a sheep and woolpack, suggesting she was a trader in her own right. On another, John Fortey – the single biggest donor to the church – is shown richly dressed in a fur-lined gown, and a pendant that bears his 'woolmark', the signature stamp of each trader. Clearly keen to win favour with the Almighty, Fortey's will not only donated a huge sum of money to finish the church renovations but also bequeathed cash to every single prisoner in Gloucester Castle, £200 to make cloth for the poor, a bursary to support a student at Oxford for four years, £1 each to eighty poor women on their marriage, and ½ mark (around six shillings and ten pence in the currency of the day) each towards the upkeep of 120 other local churches.[21]

Regardless of the rationales behind the architectural bequests, few can argue with the results: England's wool churches are some of the most celebrated examples of medieval craftsmanship and architecture. In addition to St Peter and St Paul in Northleach, among the finest examples include: St John the Baptist in both Cirencester and Burford, St James's in Chipping Campden and St Mary's in Chipping Norton; in Norfolk, St Agnes in Cawston, St Peter's in Walpole, St Peter and St Paul's in Salle; and in Suffolk, St Edmund's at Southwold, Holy Trinity at Long Melford and St Peter and St Paul at Lavenham – to name but a handful. There are literally hundreds of them. The county of Norfolk, for example, has 635 alone.

The construction, and interior design, of the wool churches supported the livelihoods of hundreds of craftspeople, many of whom travelled from across Europe to work on the buildings. Legions of stonemasons and sculptors, stained-glass makers, embroiderers, carpenters, painters, gilders and metalworkers were kept in employment thanks to the profits made from the wool trade. Far from immigration being a recent phenomenon, there are more than a thousand records of foreign workers living in medieval Suffolk alone – one record, from 1483,[22] for example, shows two Flemish craftsmen, painter Anthony Lammoson and sculptor Henry Phelypp, living in Long Melford, working under the patronage of Sir John Clopton, a wealthy wool merchant who was financing the demolition and rebuilding of Holy Trinity Church.

Only a few years earlier, Sir John had been arrested along with five others - John de Vere, Earl of Oxford, his son Aubrey de Vere, Sir Thomas Tuddenham, Sir William Tyrrell and Sir John Montgomery. All five were sent to the Tower of London by Edward IV for writing to the wife of the former King Henry VI - an act of treason after the Yorkist Edward had deposed the Lancastrian Henry. While all the rest were beheaded, Sir John's neck was spared. Quite why Sir John was allowed to live when the others were executed isn't clear, but it is likely that wool money talked. Clopton was also a huge benefactor to the local parish, an executor for many other wealthy men's financial affairs, and the sheriff of both Norfolk and Suffolk.[23] In medieval England, it seems, wool could buy not only a place in the afterlife but some security in this one; or, in the words of an inscription at the home of a wool merchant from Newark - 'I thank God, and ever shall, It is the sheepe that payed for all.'[24]

II

SHEEP DEVOUR
PEOPLE

Ghost ships, green cheese and 'Get off my land'

In May 1349 a ship carrying sacks of wool ran aground off the coast of Norway. When curious locals boarded the stricken vessel they found, to their horror, that the entire crew was dead. Having set off from London, bound for Bergen, one by one the sailors had died in feverish, blistered agony. Little did the Norwegian villagers know that as soon as they had boarded the shipwreck, their dreadful fate had also been sealed.

The Black Death swept across Europe, decimating towns and villages in its wake, helped in no small measure by the merchant ships that carried raw wool, finished cloth and the deadly bacterium *Yersinia pestis* back and forward between Europe's busiest ports. By the time the plague had exhausted its mission, it had killed around half Europe's population. And in the hundred or so years that followed the Black Death, sheep became even more important to the rural economy of England.

The effects of the plague had been devasting, wiping out entire communities. And while few places were left untouched by its deadly grip, certain areas suffered particularly catastrophic declines in population, especially those areas that had frequent contact with the Continent, such as East Anglia. The town of Great Yarmouth in Norfolk, for example, lost over seven thousand of its nine thousand or so inhabitants in one year alone.[1] Romney Marsh, further south, was also badly hit. Smugglers may have brought the disease to this quiet corner of southeast England – out went the raw wool to France and, along with their contraband, in came the rats and the plague. Some of the hamlets and villages on the Romney Marsh were simply deserted or decimated, never to be reoccupied.

In Romney Marsh, and across much of Britain, the population drop caused by the Black Death meant that there often simply weren't enough people left behind to cultivate the land. The lucky few who did survive also found they could command higher wages. Government and great landowners started to become increasingly concerned about the growing power of the rural workforce – poor folk were clearly getting ideas above their station.

In England, the Statute of Labourers of 1351 attempted to fix wages at their 1345 level; the French government followed suit with similar legislation only a few years later. The idea that peasants could hold any power over the privileged turned traditional notions on their head, unsettling the upper strata of fourteenth-century society. John Gower, friend of Chaucer, reminisced about the good old days before social boundaries were so roundly trampled:

The labourers of olden times were not accustomed to eat wheat bread; their bread was made of brans and of other corn, and their drink was water. Then cheese and milk were as a feast to them rarely had they any other feast than this. Their clothing was plain grey. Then was the world of such folk well-ordered in its estate.

One of the most bizarre outcomes of this period was the strengthening of 'sumptuary laws', rules and regulations designed to restrict what people bought and wore. The idea was clear – what you consumed marked out your social rank. Clothing, in particular, showed status; how confusing, argued the medieval elite, to have newly monied 'lower classes' wearing luxurious, 'upper class' garments. The Statute Concerning Diet and Apparel, introduced in England in 1363, is almost hysterical in its desire to keep people in their socially defined boxes; while lords with lands worth over £1,000 (just under a million in today's money) could wear pretty much what they liked, every other stratum of society was subject to restrictions based on wealth.

With every drop in personal riches, the permitted clothes became dowdier. For most people, furs and precious fabrics were banned – no weasel fur, ermine, clothing decorated with precious stones, no cloth of gold, no silk and so on. At the bottom of the heap, 'Carters, ploughmen, drivers of the plough, oxherds, cowherds, shepherds, and all other people owning less than 40s. of goods and chattels shall only wear blanket and russet worth no more than 12d. and girdles of linen according to their estate.'[2] Russet was a coarse, cheap, brown-grey woollen cloth – wearing it would instantly mark you out as poor, but for some it became a badge of piety; priests belonging to mendicant orders such as the Franciscans would wear russet as a sign of their asceticism. Some three hundred years later, during the English Civil War, Oliver Cromwell, Parliamentary general and future Lord Protector of England, remarked pointedly in a letter to Sir William Spring, 'I had rather have a plain russet-coated Captain, that knows what he fights for, and loves what he knows, than that you call a Gentleman and is nothing else.'[3]

The marked reduction of the population also permanently changed the landscape of Britain. Sheep farming was one of the only types of agriculture that didn't need much labour – one shepherd could tend to vast areas of pasture. Numbers of sheep increased dramatically – on the Bishop of Winchester's estate, for example, there were 22,500 sheep in 1348. By the mid-1350s it had increased to 30,000 and would peak at nearly 35,000 by 1369.[4]

But the biggest change in both the appearance and economics of the English landscape came about as a result of enclosure. Since the Roman invasion, the English countryside had been enthusiastically farmed in places. By the time of the Domesday Book, around 8 million acres of land were tilled; unlike the rest of northwest Europe, where huge areas of wilderness remained intact, much of central and southern England was occupied and 'it was difficult to travel for more than half a day without making human contact.'[5] Arable farming was particularly important, but few parcels of land were owned outright by anyone but the king. The king gave certain rights to local lords, who then rented out land to tenants. In return for rent and labour, the tenant had legal rights to farm the land and access to common areas such as woodland, where he could exercise certain rights. These common rights might include the right to fish, cut turf for fuel, take fallen wood for burning, extract walling stone or lime for building, turn pigs out to pannage (woodland floor grazing) and graze livestock, including sheep, on common pastureland.

The ancient 'open-field' system operated on a basis of communal use – each lord had an area of land called a manor, which was divided into fields and then into narrow strips of land. Each tenant would have a mixture of strips, some on good land, some of poor land, so that – in an ideal world – each tenant had roughly the same amount of cultivatable land. The fields and strips had little or nothing by way of boundaries – no walls, ditches or high hedges – and were looked after by families or individuals. One strip might be used to grow wheat, another to grow hay for winter feed, and another for grazing. For centuries this system of shared fields persisted; tenants would hope to grow enough to subsist and, in a good year, exchange any surplus for goods or money. Villagers would come together to plough, harvest and settle any disputes or areas of common interest. Without romanticizing what would have been a tough, precarious existence as a small-scale farmer, life under the open-field system was at least relatively self-sufficient and egalitarian.

With the population in tatters after the Black Death, wages rising and the demand for British wool showing few signs of letting up, great landlords, and sometimes groups of farmers, began enclosing parcels of land to create large fields for sheep grazing. Boundaries went up and rights that had been exercised for hundreds of years were swept away by the effective privatization of land. The process was piecemeal and informal at first, and sometimes even carried out with the cooperation of a group of farming tenants, but a notion had been set in place that was to permanently alter how people viewed the land; access became a privilege, not a right.

The first onslaught of enclosure came between the fourteenth and seventeenth centuries, leaving thousands of people dispossessed. While some peasants sought redress in the courts many others felt compelled to take direct action. Combined with the effects of decades of high taxes, inflation, famine, plague, war and a belief that wealth inequality was against God's teachings, there were a number of ill-fated popular uprisings including Wat Tyler's Peasants' Revolt of 1381, Jack Cade's Rebellion of 1450 and Kett's Rebellion of 1549. Many of the names of those involved in these uprisings are still celebrated as radical heroes today, but we rarely hear of John Reynolds, hero of the Midland Revolt of 1607.

The story begins, as all good ones do, with a pantomime villain. Sir Thomas Tresham was a greedy landlord, widely hated for rampant acts of enclosure across the entire parish. Ignoring pleas, and even a legal ruling against him, Tresham carried on annexing land, throwing off farmers and tenants, and replacing them with sheep. By the spring of 1607, Thomas Tresham was dead, as was his son Francis (who was executed for his role in the Gunpowder Plot), but the family's penchant for enclosure continued unabated, and the people of Northamptonshire had had enough. Their hero came in the unlikely form of John Reynolds, an uneducated tinker with an unshakeable belief that God was on his side. On his belt he wore a leather pouch, the mysterious contents of which were secret but, he claimed, would protect his followers from harm and secure a victory.

Trouble broke out in Rushton in April, and the following month spread to the neighbouring counties of Leicestershire and Warwickshire. In Cotesbach in Leicestershire as many as five thousand people are thought to have joined Reynolds – or 'Captain Pouch', as he became known – pulling down fences, filling in ditches and scrubbing up hedgerows in protest. Despite their enthusiasm, the rebellion was quickly quashed by the king's militia and Captain Pouch arrested. He was charged and sentenced to the punishment reserved especially for traitors – to be hanged, drawn and quartered.

On his death, the leather pouch was opened. The secret contents, which had galvanized the entire rebellion, turned out to be just a lump of old, mouldy cheese.

The effects of enclosure on the poor were often catastrophic. Few were compensated for their loss of access to common land and the traditional peasantry were replaced by an agricultural proletariat dependent on waged labour. In the old open-field system, tenants remained, for good or ill, the paternalistic responsibility of the lord of the manor; not only did it make sound economic sense for him to keep his tenants alive and relatively healthy, as his wealth came from their efforts, but it also afforded him the social cachet of the benevolent landlord.

The church had also, until then, seen it as their moral duty to care for the poor and oppressed, the widows, orphans, infirm and elderly. Monasteries and church hospitals routinely gave alms to the needy, whether able-bodied or not. Poverty wasn't seen as a moral failing, it was simply the result of unfortunate circumstances, and certainly not something that could be eradicated by punishment. The toxic combination of the enclosures, the plague, the demise of the monasteries and a rising landless population led to a new class of poor, the 'wandering ones': people who went from parish to parish, town to village, village to town, searching desperately for work. What was different, however, was how the government planned to deal with them.

In the past, begging was regarded as acceptable – it was

one of the only legitimate ways the unemployed poor could survive. Indeed, those at the time who were familiar with the teachings of the Bible would have known that the destitute were to be protected. The gospel according to Luke quoted Jesus as saying to his disciples: 'Blessed be ye poor: for yours is the kingdom of God.' While Isaiah 10: 1–2 stated: 'Woe to the legislators of infamous laws, to those who issue tyrannical decrees, refuse justice to the unfortunate and cheat the poor among my people of their rights, who make widows their prey and rob the orphan.'

The Statute of Labourers, which had capped workers' wages after the Black Death, however, provided explicit instructions about what to do with the able-bodied beggars – they were to be seized and put to work. This was the first time public policy had divided the poor into the 'deserving' and 'undeserving', a notion that still permeates social policy today.

Subsequent acts of Parliament concerned with poor relief built on this notion of punishing the 'idle', those beggars and vagabonds who, in society's eyes, chose not work. A raft of Vagrancy Acts between 1495 and 1597 laid out a set of brutal disincentives against begging or vagrancy. The 1531 Vagabonds Act, for example, made it clear who could do what; only the 'aged and impotent' could beg and even then, they needed a letter of authorization to do so and could only beg in a certain parish or area. Those found begging outside their 'zone' or without an official letter faced the stocks and the humiliation of being stripped naked from the middle upwards and whipped. And that was if you were a *legitimate* beggar. Any man, woman or child 'being in whole and mighty in body, and able to labour'[6] who was caught begging faced harsh treatment from the local justice of the peace:

> Every such justice etc by their discretions shall cause every such idle person to be had to the next market-town, or to other place most convenient, and there be tied to the end of a cart naked, and beaten with whips throughout the same town or other place, till his body be bloody by reason of such whipping; and after such punishment he shall be enjoined upon his oath to return forthwith the next straight way to the place where he was born, or where he last dwelled the space of three years, and there put himself to labour like as a true man oweth to do.[7]

Under the subsequent 1547 Vagrancy Act, passed by Edward VI, able-bodied beggars were branded with the letter 'V' and legally enslaved for two years. Their masters were required to feed them bread and water but had the freedom to beat, whip or chain their charges as they saw fit. Child vagrants, without the consent of their parents, were also bought and sold into service and held until adulthood. While the slavery element of the 1547 Act made it unpopular with the general population, and it was repealed in 1550, a subsequent 1572 Act replaced indenture with state-sanctioned torture: 'all vagabonds to be grievously whipped and burned through the gristle of the right ear with a hot iron an inch in diameter.' These were no idle threats; beggars would be punished. In 1630, for example, the poet John Taylor counted sixty whipping posts – known locally as 'Posts of Reformation' – on London's streets alone.[8]

The brutality of the early poor relief system and the eviction of peasant farmers from the land for sheep didn't go unnoticed by contemporary writers and commentators. Thomas More's *Utopia*, published more than five hundred years ago, in 1516, was astonishingly critical for its time. More saw the mass poverty created by the enclosures and the greed of the wealthy as a direct affront to Christian principles: 'your sheep that were wont to be so meek and tame, and so small eaters, now [...] become so great devourers and so wild, that they eat up, and swallow down the very men themselves. They consume, destroy, and devour whole fields, houses, and cities.'[9] It's radical stuff, not least because it aims its fire directly at those at the very highest levels of society who live, More complains, like parasites on the labour of others. It cannot be right, he argues, that 'one insatiable glutton and accursed plague of his native land may join field to field and surround many thousand acres with one fence'.

Few areas of the country escaped the effects of the land grab. Shakespeare even found himself embroiled in an enclosure scandal; the Bard and his cousin Thomas Greene were modest landowners in Stratford, earning tithe income from their fields. Two local wealthy men, John Combe and Arthur Mainwaring, attempted to enclose land that included Shakespeare and Greene's plots. Shakespeare and Greene would be compensated, insisted the proposers of the scheme, but both the Stratford Corporation and Greene objected, worried the enclosures would add to growing local unemployment and push up grain prices.

Although the enclosures initially went ahead, to the community's despair, the scheme eventually faltered and was more or less abandoned. And, despite the fact that Shakespeare had, in many ways, championed the dispossessed and landless in plays such as *King Lear*, when push came to shove he chose to protect his own interests. Shakespeare, unbeknown to Greene, had made a private pact with Mainwaring that ensured he wouldn't lose out financially, whatever the outcome.[10]

Few agree on the long-term effects of enclosures. For some, they represent a national trauma, a key moment when a large swathe of society became permanently dispossessed or, as the historian E. P. Thompson argued, 'a plain enough case of class robbery'. Meticulous manorial records from the fifteenth and sixteenth centuries detail, with painstaking clarity, the rising number of sheep kept by landowners, but few accounts give any qualitative detail about the human suffering that must have accompanied these changes. As one historian notes: 'If a village was already small and poorly located, and if a local landlord was sufficiently determined and aggressive, enclosure could result in the extinction of the community.'[11]

For other social commentators, enclosures represent a necessary step in the development of agriculture, one that spelled an end to the grinding poverty and uncertainty of subsistence farming. Without doubt, enclosures made land more productive, allowed the population of Britain to increase, and set the foundations for the Industrial Revolution, but at an enormous human cost. Whichever view you hold, by the nineteenth century, there was little unenclosed land left and what remained was largely rough mountain pasture, forest and village greens. Today, the legacy of sheep enclosure lives on – half of England is owned by just 25,000 landowners, less than 1 per cent of its population.

The Highland Clearances of the late eighteenth and early nineteenth centuries constitute one of the darkest episodes in the history of enclosure. By the middle of the eighteenth century, the urge to enclose English land for sheep grazing was ebbing away. Much of the land had already been fenced off and many of those displaced by its effects had had drifted towards the towns and cities in search of factory work. The population was also rising rapidly, requiring more land for food production. Wool was still big business, but the growth of the cotton industry, fed by cheap imports from India and the slave plantations of the United States, was beginning to challenge wool's dominance of the market.

Greedy eyes turned towards the Scottish Highlands. The Act of Union of 1707 had merged England and Scotland into the Kingdom of Great Britain. Scotland's extensive, mountainous pastures had been occupied by Highland clans for centuries, but this proved little obstacle to those landowners and businessmen eager to replace people with sheep. There was also a political motive; the British establishment were keen to 'cleanse' Scotland of the clans who had resisted the union and who had supported the 'Jacobite' revolts of 1715 and 1745–6, which had attempted to restore the Stuart dynasty in place of Britain's new Hanoverian monarchy.

In a century-long process that has become known as the 'Clearances', tens of thousands of Highlanders – men, women and children – were thrown off their traditional holdings, often violently, to make way for livestock. At first, many families were relocated to barren land by the sea, where they were expected to make a living from fishing, quarrying or harvesting seaweed for the soap and glassmaking industries. In 1793, for example, the inhabitants of three inland valleys in Caithness were sent to Badbea, a remote and inhospitable scrap of land, perched on top of a steep cliff on the county's southeastern coast. The women were expected to make cloth, the men to fish for herring, and each family was promised a small plot to tend. In reality, conditions were impossible – people were forced to clear their own plots and build houses from the stones and rocks lying around. Such was the ferocity of the weather, reports from the time talk of livestock and children having to be tethered to posts to stop them being blown into the sea.

Few Highlanders left willingly; many were literally burnt out of house and home. Some even perished in the flames. In his book *The Highland Clearances* (1963) John Prebble collected some of the first-hand accounts of the trauma inflicted on locals:

Betsy MacKay was 16 and she lived at the river's edge by Skail. 'Our family was very reluctant to leave,' she remembered, 'and stayed for some time, but the burning party came round and set fire to our house at both ends, reducing to ashes whatever remained within the walls. The people had to escape for their lives, some of them losing all their clothes except what they had on their backs. The people were told they could go where they liked, provided they did not encumber the land that was by rights their own.'[12]

In another account, Grace MacDonald, then nineteen, shelters on a hill, watching her township burn.

Grace [...] waited there a day and a night, watching Sellar's men sporting about the flames. When a terrified cat sprang from a burning house, it was seized and thrown back, and thrown back again until it died there. 'There was no mercy or pity shown to young or old,' said Grace Macdonald. 'All had to clear away, and those who could not get their effects removed in time had it burnt before their eyes.'[13]

Some landlords offered 'assisted emigration' for the Highlanders, paying the passage for families to be shipped off to America and, later on, Australia. In 1826, the Inner Hebridean Isle of Rùm was cleared of its 300 inhabitants, who were packed off to Nova Scotia. While the owner of Rùm had paid £5 for each passenger to be transported, he clearly knew he was getting a bargain; the entire community only paid £300 in annual rent, while the single sheep farmer who remained on the island with his 8,000 sheep was charged £900 a year.[14] Rùm had been occupied for thousands of years – since 7500 BC – and yet in the space of just one year it had all but been emptied. On leaving his ancestral land, a 'shepherd of Rhum, John McMaister, recalled, "the wild outcries of the men and the heart-breaking wails of the women and children, filling all the air between the mountainous shores", as the people were chased on to the ships for Nova Scotia – at the beginning of winter, too. The ships were, with dreadful irony, called the *Dove of Harmony* and the *Highland Lad*.'[15]

On at least one occasion, tenants were even handcuffed and physically forced aboard awaiting ships. In 1851, 1,500 inhabitants of Barra, in the Outer Hebrides, were duped into attending a compulsory meeting about land rents. Instead, the Barra people were overpowered and forced to board ships waiting to take them to Canada. As people were frogmarched onboard, those that resisted were handcuffed. Any that broke free and made a run for it were chased down by dogs and captured.

Only a few Barra residents escaped the clutches of the pursuing estate officers by fleeing to the hills, including two young girls, aged twelve and fourteen. Their parents, along with the rest of the islanders, set sail without them. When the ships finally reached Atlantic shores, life was no better. One Ontario newspaper – the *Dundas Warder* – reported in the same year, 'We have been pained beyond measure for some time past, to witness in our streets so many unfortunate Highland emigrants, apparently destitute of any means of subsistence, and many of them sick from want and other attendant causes.'[16]

For a while, the new Highland sheep farms were a success. Up until the early 1870s, pretty much every area of the British agricultural sector was booming; or as one commentator put it, 'everything appeared to be going the British farmer's way.'[17] Sheep farming was doing particularly well – wool prices almost doubled between the 1850s and 1860s, largely thanks to a 'cotton famine' brought on by the economic and social disruption of the American Civil War. It was, according to one Highland land agent, a halcyon period, when 'landlords and sheep farmers alike [...] waxed fat and prosperous'.[18]

It wasn't to last. At the end of the nineteenth century, the

Highland sheep industry was to be decimated by a toxic mix of greed, bad luck and foreign competition. Putting short-term profit before long-term sustainability, many sheep estates were overstocked; the land simply couldn't cope. The fertility of hill pastureland plummeted, and, while some farmers reduced the numbers of sheep they kept, others simply pressed ahead, maintaining stocks at previous levels. With not enough grass to eat, the sheep failed to thrive, declined in quality, and became much more susceptible to disease.

The weather also didn't help – during the 1870s and 1880s, a series of brutal winters hit the Highlands. During the worst of these – in 1879–80 – some areas of Scotland saw protracted and heavy snowfall for three solid months, leaving sheep farmers hand-feeding their stock and losing many to the drifts. The real blow, however, came from America, Australia and New Zealand. These newly settled lands had embraced large-scale agricultural production and this, combined with rapid improvements in long-distance shipping, helped them to aggressively undercut British prices. Between the 1850s and the 1880s, wool imports had increased five-fold. By the mid-1890s, 70 per cent of all the wool being used in Great Britain came from overseas.[19]

In the 1880s, a folklorist named Alexander Mackenzie published a book in which he claimed to have collected the prophecies of the 'Brahan Seer'. Doubts have been raised as to whether the Brahan Seer ever existed, and some claim that he is an invention of Mackenzie's; whatever the truth of the matter, his predictions make for uncanny reading:

> The day will come when [...] sheep shall become so numerous that the bleating of the one shall be heard by the other from Conchra in Lochalsh to Bun-da-loch in Kintail, they shall be at their height in price, and henceforth will go back and deteriorate, until they disappear altogether [...] The ancient proprietors of the soil shall give place to strange merchant proprietors, and the whole Highlands will become one huge deer forest; the whole country will be so utterly desolated and depopulated that the crow of a cock shall not be heard north of Druim-Uachdair.

Meanwhile, over in America, another traditional group of sheep farmers was also being displaced. The Churro breed of sheep came to southwestern America with the Spanish conquistadors in the early 1500s. Within a hundred years, the breed had been embraced by the indigenous Navajo, who loved its hardiness and adaptability to the arid native lands of New Mexico, Arizona, Colorado and Utah.

The Navajo – who call themselves *Diné*, or 'the people' – prized the Churro for their lean meat and low maintenance but also their wool, which had long lustrous fibres perfectly suited to hand spinning and weaving. The fleece was also naturally low in lanolin, making it easy to wash in an environment where every drop of water was precious. The indigenous people quickly became expert wool crafters, turning the Churro fibre into coveted rugs, saddle blankets, coats and other clothes. Soon the sustenance, success and spirituality of the Navajo people became intertwined with the Churro sheep, which they believed to be a gift from the gods.

In 1863, however, the Navajo were declared enemies of the state. The US military, led by frontiersman Kit Carson, were sent to suppress the Navajo, with strict instructions to destroy their crops, orchards and flocks. After slaughtering countless sheep, the US army then forced 9,000 Navajo to walk from their homeland to an internment camp 300 miles (480 kilometres) away. Scores of men, women and children died on what has become known as 'The Long Walk'.

Those Navajos that evaded capture went into hiding with the remnants of their flocks and over the next few decades of careful management were able to rebuild Churro numbers, along with other breeds of sheep. By end of the 1920s, the Navajo people – who had been allowed to return to their ancestral lands – owned nearly half a million sheep.

The good times weren't to last. During the Great Depression of the 1930s, the US government came calling again. Congress believed the Navajo had too many sheep on their land and enforced a mandatory 'stock reduction' – over the next decade nearly half of the Navajo flock was slaughtered, bringing the indigenous economy to its knees and leaving the Churro on the verge of extinction. The mass butchery of flocks traumatized the Navajo, who continue to recite stories of federal agents shooting sheep in their pens or chasing Churro off cliff edges. Piles of seventy-year-old sheep bones still litter many of the reservations.

The story doesn't have an entirely unhappy ending, however. In the early 1970s, a Utah professor began the Navajo Sheep Project. His plan was to build up numbers from the handful of sheep that survived. Today, there are several thousand Churros, but the sheep and Navajo who farm them face a different challenge. Thanks to climate change and the constant threat of droughts faced by many regions of southwestern America, a native way of life sits in the balance.

12

SPINNING A YARN

Fisherman's jumpers, men in tights
and a famous execution

During the long reign of Elizabeth I, the Channel island of Guernsey exported a staggering number of hand-knitted woollen stockings. Islanders – often women and children working from home – were commissioned by middlemen to mass-produce fine, knitted hosiery for an eager European market, including the English royal household.

Both men and women clamoured to wear knitted tights; most popular of all were cannions, or *bas a canon** – manly pull-ups worn with knee-length breeches and decorated with lace and ribbon. Queen Elizabeth paid 20 shillings for Guernsey wool stockings embellished with silk (the equivalent of twenty days' wages for a skilled tradesman). Mary, Queen of Scots, wouldn't be seen dead in anything else; she insisted on a pair of white Guernsey knitted stockings for the day of her execution.

---

* In Guernsey, cannions were called *'bas de canons'*, according to letters sent between Matthew and Michael de Saumarez in the 1600s. Source: www.museums.gov.gg

The Channel Islands were particularly well placed for exporting knitted goods. During the 1400s Guernsey merchants had clubbed together to pay for a local militia to help resist French invasion.* In return, the merchants asked the king to issue a royal grant enabling islanders to import English wool at advantageous rates. Over the next few centuries, the Channel Islands also found themselves in the middle of an extensive trade network that stretched between Europe and newly established, far-flung colonies such as Newfoundland. Warm woollen clothes were needed for the crews of privateering galleons as well as an ever-expanding number of naval seamen and fishermen, all of whom undertook long, arduous sea journeys.

By the mid-nineteenth century the blue Guernsey jumper had become a staple item of clothing for men in the fishing industry across Britain. In many places, such as Cornwall and Yorkshire, the Guernsey name mutated into the 'gansey', but the design remained similar from region to region. It's knitted 'in the round', like a big tube without seams, making it possible to unravel sections and reknit them, or recycle the

* The Royal Guernsey Militia is thought to be one of the oldest British regiments. Guernsey, throughout its history, was under constant threat of invasion. In 1203, King John ordered that the elite of the island should provide 'sufficiency of men and money to defend the Island from the enemy'. Over the following centuries, Guernsey was subject to frequent raids, mostly by the French, but the island remained loyal to the British crown. To show its gratitude the crown often waived taxes and custom duties on trade.

wool if the jumper is beyond repair. The front and back is identical, so it can be worn back to front if a patch wears thin (it's also said that fisherman could wipe their hands on their jumpers and simply turn them around). Gussets under the arm stop the sweater from being strained when a fisherman is pulling hard to land a catch, and both the body and sleeves are knitted slightly short, to stop them getting caught in the ropes or netting.

The knitters used wool that was traditionally unwashed; leaving the lanolin in the wool helped keep it waterproof for the men at sea. The fact that Guernseys are traditionally blue was down to a peculiarity of natural dying; woad, a popular medieval dye, was one of the only ones that didn't require a fleece to be scoured first. This meant the yarn could take the blue colour without losing any of its natural water-resistant qualities.

One of the defining features of the Guersney or gansey is the pattern, sometimes applied to the whole sweater but more often kept to the chest and arms. The designs are based around familiar fishing imagery – ropes, cables, herringbones, netting, ladders, chains – and often particular to a parish or region. In England's northeast, for example, traditional fishing communities such as Robin Hood's Bay, Flamborough, Filey, Staithes, Scarborough and Whitby may share the same small stretch of coastline, but each community's gansey has its own distinct, unmistakable pattern written into the fabric.

Craft and hyper-locality often go hand in hand, families passing tweaks and idiosyncratic patterns of making down from generation to generation; there's sometimes no practical reason, just the pleasure of creating a signature, tell-tale piece. For fishing communities, the distinctiveness of a woollen sweater may have helped identify a body should an unfortunate fisherman fall victim to the sea. It's an idea that folklore enthusiasts love to repeat – nothing grips the attention like a gruesome tale of body washed up on a beach – but textile historians are cautious. Patterns on fishermen's jumpers were also passed between places, often as a result of 'herring girls' who would follow the seasonal migration of herring fleets around the country, knitting in their quieter moments and sharing patterns with other local women.

Folklore has a way of becoming fact if repeated often enough, as is the case with another famous fishing jumper – the Aran. The Irish poet Seamus Heaney once described the Aran Islands, across the mouth of Galway Bay in Ireland, as 'three stepping stones out of Europe./ Anchored like hulls at the dim horizon'.[1] Rocky, remote and startlingly beautiful, the islands give their name to Aran sweaters, those chunky limestone-white cable knits that have become a recognized symbol of Irish authenticity and kinship. Tourist shops will tell you that the sweaters contain special patterns or stitches that are unique to ancient families or clans, dating back hundreds of years. People, especially those with Irish ancestry, travel

224

far and wide to purchase, and wear, a slice of their Celtic heritage. And yet, for the most part, this idea of clan patterns is pure fiction.

There's been plenty of academic wrangling over the authenticity of Aran knitwear. What emerges is as much a story about migrant narratives as the history of knitting patterns. It all starts with a tale not dissimilar to the Guernsey or gansey sweater:

> The basic narrative goes like this: a fisherman goes out onto the dangerous Atlantic Ocean, wearing a jumper knitted by his female relations. Trying to earn a living, he is lost at sea. His battered body, once washed ashore, is unrecognizable. His jumper, however, identifies the corpse as belonging to one particular family, who can then claim and bury his body.[2]

Many people in Ireland know that the story is, indeed, just that. And yet the myth persists, embellished and elaborated by tourism and the wool trade, especially across the Atlantic. The myth behind the Aran jumper probably comes from a more recent time and the words of Irish playwright J. M. Synge (1871–1909), who wrote extensively about the fishing communities of the Aran Islands. In one of his tragedies, *Riders to the Sea*, Synge describes a moment when a woman identifies her drowned brother from the unmistakable stitches on his woolly socks. In the 1963 book *Aran: Islands of Legend*, the myth is further oversewn by author and entrepreneur Pádraig Ó Síocháin, who writes with great confidence that 'the Aran gansey has always been an unfailing source of identification of Islandmen lost at sea', despite there being little evidence that this was the case. Interestingly, the author of the book also owned Galway Bay Products, who made and exported Aran knitwear. Thanks to Ó Síocháin's canny instinct for marketing and the value of a product's heritage, however invented, sales of Aran jumpers and cardigans rocketed. Countries with large Irish emigrant communities couldn't get enough of these 'ancient' sweaters, especially the United States, Canada and Australia. Creating a romantic backstory for the Aran jumper – which was more about repackaging local history and heritage – spoke to a diasporic audience longing to reconnect with their ancestral past, however mythologized that might be. As one Irish historian points out:

Not only is there no evidence to support the idea that our ancestors knitted special 'clan stitches', the Aran sweaters' tradition is actually relatively new. If it has been handed down the generations at all, it can have been only two or three generations because, as any time traveller would confirm, if you stepped onto one of the three Aran Islands 100 years ago, it is highly unlikely you would encounter locals wearing what we would recognise as Aran sweaters.[3]

The phenomenal manufacturing success of the Aran jumper owes more to a late nineteenth-century initiative – the Congested Districts Board – a British government policy with the intention of alleviating poverty in the west and northwest of Ireland. It was part of an approach clumsily described by the Chief Secretary for Ireland as 'killing Home Rule with kindness' – though Irish nationalists took a rather different view. Local women were encouraged to pick up their needles and knit furiously – fishing and sheep farming were already well established on Aran but times were hard, so making a sideways step into knitting fishermen's ganseys with local materials seemed a crafty move.

The Aran jumper as a symbol of Irish kinship and heritage clearly struck a chord. During the 1950s and 1960s, it became the go-to uniform for the Irish folk music scene, sported by such much-loved singers such as Tommy Makem and the Clancy Brothers. Even Hollywood came calling – when Grace Kelly, Marilyn Monroe and Steve McQueen pulled on their cream pullovers, it elevated the Aran jumper from icon of rural Irish life to covetable item of knitwear that spoke of home, heart and heritage.

What's perhaps less well known is that Aran jumpers also became linked to the scandal of the Magdalene Laundries, institutions for 'fallen women' who included single mothers, abused girls and orphans. Such was the success of the Aran jumper in the early twentieth century that some of the work was outsourced to the Laundries, to be carried out by an impoverished, exploited workforce. It's one of history's cruel ironies that Aran jumpers, which represented all that was wholesome and deep-rooted about Irish kinship and domestic life, were sometimes made by women who had been separated from their own families or had their own children forcibly removed. Incredibly, the Laundries – which were operated by Roman Catholic orders from the mid 1700s onwards – only closed in the late twentieth century amid media revelations of sexual, psychological and physical abuse.

Reinventing a past through the story of wool isn't confined to Aran jumpers. Interestingly, almost the same scenario exists with the Icelandic sweater, a garment that is often presented as being traditional and authentically ancient, lovingly hand-crafted by local women from the wool of native sheep and following centuries-old patterns. In reality, the sweater's popularity seems to be closely linked to periods in modern history when Iceland needed to reassert its sense of identity and national self-confidence.

While knitting has been in Iceland for at least four hundred years, the iconic sweater, or *lopapeysa*, seems to have emerged in the mid-twentieth century and coincided with a time when factory-made clothes and imported goods were starting to displace older hand-knitted textiles. In the same way that William Morris and the Arts and Crafts movement in Britain tried to recapture the spirit of hand-crafted, artisan objects at the end of the nineteenth century, Icelanders began to search for ways to reignite traditional knitting skills using local wool. It also coincided with an important political moment for Iceland, when the island finally severed all ties with Denmark and declared itself an independent republic in 1944.

Icelanders, keen to nation-build and reconstruct traditional values, needed a symbol of cultural heritage. The *lopapeysa* (*lopa* means 'wool', and *peysa* 'sweater') embodied everything Iceland wanted to be – moderate, industrious and self-sufficient.[4] The knitting patterns of the *lopapeysa*, far from being handed down from generation to generation, were a glorious hotch-potch of genuine early Icelandic textile patterns, newly invented designs, and styles copied from other Nordic countries and further afield. It's interesting to note that the *lopapeysa* enjoyed a second wave of popularity after the 2008 banking collapse, when once again Iceland had to return to its roots; textile historian Kathleen Donlan notes in her exploration of Icelandic national identity, 'knitting provided Icelanders (literally and metaphorically) an opportunity to take the difficult times into their own hands and produce something of value.'[5]

'Invention of tradition' is an idea that was first put forward by British historians Eric Hobsbawm and Terence Ranger in their 1983 book of the same name. In it, they argue that many of the grand traditions that cultures love to celebrate are often surprisingly recent. What's more, these traditions are often invented to help bolster feelings of national identity or belonging. At times of crisis, migration or sweeping change, the desire to hold on to, and reinforce, these 'traditions' becomes ever stronger.

Perhaps nowhere is this better expressed than in the invention of ancient Scottish clan tartans. Tartan, without question, has become one of the most evocative, potent symbols of Scotland and its heritage. And yet the history of this woollen cloth is a tangle of genuine antiquity and extraordinary, barefaced fabrication. Fact, half-truths and fiction have become interwoven, but to unpick the threads we must first go back to tartan's very beginnings.

The earliest piece of tartan found in Scotland is astonishingly old – around 1,700 years old, in fact. The Falkirk Tartan, in the National Museum of Scotland, at first glance appears unremarkable – just a small, 2.7-inch (seven-centimetre) scrap of fabric used as a makeshift stopper on a pot. The jar contained nearly two thousand Roman coins, but it didn't belong to a Roman. Archaeologists decided that the cash was probably a bribe made to a local Celtic leader on the promise that his tribe wouldn't attack the Roman army as it retreated south, tail between its legs.

Tartan had been worn for thousands of years by the Celts,

not just in Scotland but across Europe and Scandinavia. In fact, the oldest example of tartan ever found was discovered in Western China on the mummified remains of a European, who was clearly very far from home, and died around 1000 BC. The Greek historian Diodorus Siculus, writing sometime around 50 BC, makes a note of Celtic dress sense:

> The clothing they wear is striking – shirts which have been dyed and embroidered in varied colours, and breeches, which they call in their tongue bracae; and they wear striped coats, fastened by a buckle on the shoulder, heavy for winter wear and light for summer, in which are set checks, close together and of varied hues.[6]

Romans also spoke of local tribes wearing tartan-like fabric, but even then there was no indication that particular patterns linked to particular groups; designs and the colours they used from this time right through to the introduction of exotic dyes in the eighteenth century would have been based on what was available locally, such as native lichens, heather or tree bark. Certain patterns may have been linked to particular weavers in an area, but it wasn't uncommon for Highlanders to mix and match tartan patterns, even in the same outfit. The Falkirk Tartan, for example, only has two colours, brown and white, both natural shades of the native sheep. A tartan pattern, therefore, may have been linked to a particular weaver, who supplied a specific region or set of families within a locality, but there was no definite association between clan and tartan pattern.

One of the earliest mentions of the word 'tartan' dates from 1538, when King James V purchased 'three ells of Heland Tartans' for his wife. Tartans, by that time, had become loosely associated with Highlanders, Gaelic-speaking Celtic descendants who had settled in the north of Scotland and become both feared and revered for their fighting prowess. An early woodcut from the 1630s shows Highland mercenaries clearly wearing tartan; not kilts, however, but the *philamhor* or 'great kilt', a long wide length of woollen cloth that wrapped around the body rather like an Indian sari.

Following the Glorious Revolution of 1688-9, many of the Highland clans supported the Jacobite cause, which sought to restore the deposed Catholic James II of England (and James VII of Scotland), and his Stuart descendants, to the thrones of both Scotland and England. James II's grandson - Charles Edward Stuart, or 'Bonnie Prince Charlie' - rallied support from some of the Highland clans, but at the Battle of Culloden, on 16 April 1746, the Jacobites were crushed by English and Scottish forces loyal to King George II.

Defeat took little more than an hour. The wearing of tartan, which had been such a symbol of Highland rebellion, was immediately outlawed by the English government. The ban only applied to common Highland men, however; key supporters of the English cause, including Highland regiments who had fought against the Jacobites and the upper strata of society, retained the right to wear tartan. The law was not only discriminatory but also peculiarly indiscriminate:

> There had been many combatant Lowland Jacobites. There had even been some English Jacobites in arms. But only the Scots Highlander was singled out for this calculated humiliation. The majority of clansmen had actually either kept out of the conflict, or had remained loyal to King George. Even so, the Mackays, the Grants, the Campbells, the Munros [...] and all the other clans, whose fathers, sons, brothers and husbands had fought and died for King George, were to be mortified in the same way.[7]

The tartan ban was eventually lifted in 1782. In the decades that followed there was a resurgence of Scottish nationalism and efforts to restore the spirit and culture of the Highlands were renewed (despite the fact that, at the same time, many of the Highland clans were being displaced by the Clearances). In 1822, King George IV visited Edinburgh – the first monarch to do so in over a hundred years. English–Scottish relations were still raw from the Jacobite rebellion, but some reconciliation came in the unlikely form of Walter Scott, romantic poet and author of fictionalized histories of Scotland in such novels as *Rob Roy* and *The Bride of Lammermoor*. Scott stage-managed the occasion, turning a drily formal royal visit into a joyous 'tartan fest' - a celebration of Scottish identity, Highland culture and national unity. Dress code for the occasion was clear:

> Gentlemen may appear in any uniform to which they have a right; and for those who present themselves as Highlanders, the ancient costume of their country is always sufficient dress [...] It is understood that Glengarry, Breadalbane, Huntly, and several other Chieftains, mean to attend the levee with their tail on, i.e. with a considerable attendance of their gentlemen followers. And, without doubt, this will add very greatly to the variety, gracefulness, and appropriate splendour of the scene.[8]

King George IV, never one to miss an opportunity to dress up, also slipped into his own little tartan number - a kilt that was so short it needed a pair of salmon pink tights to spare his blushes. Scott's PR exercise worked - tartan, once the woollen cloth of the rebellious Highlanders, had been tamed and turned into the national dress of the 'new' Scotland.

The idea of there being particular clan tartans, however, still hadn't taken hold; the Highland regiments had their own designs, and a handful of Scottish families had formed links with a particular pattern or designed their own, but there was no definitive guide. In the same year as George IV's visit to Scotland, two brothers emerged into high society.

John Sobieski Stuart and Charles Edward Stuart purported to be the grandsons of Bonnie Prince Charlie. They had, they claimed, discovered a fifteenth-century manuscript – *Vestiarium Scoticum*, or 'Scottish Clothing' – which contained the designs and patterns of all the 'official clan tartans' – lost in time but thankfully 'rediscovered' by the authors. In 1829 they tried to publish it in book form, but got cold feet when Walter Scott asked to see the original fifteenth-century manuscript. Scott died in 1832 and, ten years later, the brothers finally published *Vestiarium Scoticum* in all its magnificent, leather-bound glory. It was an instant hit. Society took the young men to their heart, eager to discover the traditional tartans of their forefathers. As one society lady remembers:

> Her sons were handsome men, particularly John Sobieski, who, however, had not a trace of the Stuart in his far finer face. They always wore the Highland dress, kilt and belted plaid, and looked melancholy, and spoke at times mysteriously. The effect they produced was astonishing; they were 'feted' to their hearts' content.[9]

The authors and the book, in time, were revealed to be phoney. Walter Scott had been right to doubt its authenticity back in 1829. Writing to a colleague, he not only expressed his view that he didn't believe in the legitimacy of the book, but he also didn't subscribe to the entire concept, claiming the 'idea of distinguishing the clans by their tartans is but a fashion of modern date'.[10] John Sobieski Stuart and Charles Edward Stuart were exposed as John and Charles Allen, not royal descendants from the Stuart household but two young men from Wales with fertile imaginations. It didn't seem to matter, however. The notion of clan tartans had got under high society's skin.

Queen Victoria and Prince Albert famously decked out the newly restored Balmoral Castle in wall-to-wall tartan; from curtains to carpets, dresses to children's outfits. The fashionable royal couple were so enamoured with Scotland and its symbolic fabric that they even created their own design – the Balmoral tartan. As for the Allen brothers, they returned to London in 1868. Poverty-stricken and disgraced, they continued to keep up their pretence, spending hours in the British Museum Reading Room attempting to establish their legitimacy. They spent so long in the library, it's said they even had a table reserved especially for their use where they would spend hours scribbling away with pens 'surmounted with miniature coronets in gold'.[11]

13

MILLS AND BOOM

White slavery, wool-lined coffins
and 'la maladie de Bradford'

Anyone idly flicking through the pages of the September issue of *Cosmopolitan* magazine in 1906 might have stumbled upon one particular story. It described a recent visit to New York made by an old Native American chieftain. On his tour, he was shown all the glorious sights of the city - the skyscrapers, Brooklyn Bridge, the vast shopping emporiums selling everything a person could desire. At the end of his journey, he was enthusiastically asked, 'What is the most surprising thing you have seen?' The chieftain thought for a moment and replied, slowly: 'Little children working.'[1]

And yet child labour had been the fuel that powered the Industrial Revolution, and the textile industry in particular, on both sides of the Atlantic for at least one hundred and fifty years. But to understand how we got there, we first have to go back to the late 1400s.

English exports in raw wool had reached dizzying heights during the late thirteenth and fourteenth centuries. By the end of the 1400s, however, successive taxes on the wool industry -

levied to fund the wars with France – had unintentionally forced England to develop its own handwoven cloth market. Rather than send English wool abroad to be woven into cloth, which the country then bought back at a greatly inflated price, wool merchants and entrepreneurs realized they could make their own and sell it both in England and abroad.

This burgeoning cloth industry was given a further boost by an influx of highly skilled Flemish cloth weavers; first in the fourteenth century by royal invitation – Edward III hoped the Flemish weavers could show English crafters how it was really done – and again during the sixteenth century, when Flemish Protestants fled religious persecution. Those who came settled in various regions across the country – many landed and stayed in Norfolk and Suffolk, while others ventured further, ending up in the Cotswolds, the West Country, Yorkshire and beyond.

In 1454, Parliament had declared that 'the making of cloth within all parts of the realm is the greatest occupation and living of the poor commons of this land',[2] while nearly three hundred years later, Daniel Defoe gushed, 'Be their country hot or cold, torrid or frigid, 'tis the same thing, near the Equinox or near the Pole, the English woollen manufacturer clothes them all.'[3]

Monarchs passed numerous laws to prop up the English woollen cloth market and compel its subjects to wear home-grown textiles; the Cappers Act of 1571 stated that most people must wear, on Sundays and holidays, a 'cap of wool, thicked and dressed in England [...] upon pain of forfeit for every day not wearing 3s 4d',[4] while in 1697 it was decreed that all magistrates, judges, undergraduates and law professors had to wear woollen gowns. Only a few years earlier, various Burial in Wool Acts – made between 1666 and 1680 – stated that every person must be buried in a English woollen shroud, unless the deceased had been destitute or had died as a result of the plague. It was decreed that: 'No corps should be buried in anything other than what is made of sheep's wool only; or put into any coffin lined or faced with any material but sheep's wool, on pain of forfeiture of £5.'[5]

The galloping demand for English cloth was satisfied during this time by independent workers, and their families, in a production system known as 'putting out'. Cloth merchants would supply wool to a wide network of home-based outworkers, who would then transform the yarn into finished textiles. Some outworkers spun, others wove, others dyed, others finished the fabric and so on. The cloth merchants would then travel round, collecting the semi-finished or finished products – and either pass them on to the next person in the process or take the finished lengths to sell at one of the many cloth halls across the country.

The system may have been domestic but the scale of trade was enormous, and was reflected in the grand architecture of many of the cloth halls. One stands out above them all – Halifax

Piece Hall, in West Yorkshire. Built between 1775 and 1779, the hall was erected for the express purpose of trading 'pieces' of woollen cloth.* It's an architectural wonder – a dramatic, three-tiered wedding cake of Italianate galleries overlooking a vast, 6000-square-metre open-air plaza. Traders would strike deals in the individual rooms set around the quadrangle, while being able to overlook the thrum of the crowds below.

During the 1700s Halifax was full of handweavers – in the 1720s Defoe scribbled down his impressions as he walked through the town: 'We saw houses full of lusty fellows, some at the dye-vat, some dressing the cloths, some in the loom, all hard at work and full employed. The women and children always busy carding or spinning, so that all can gain their bread even from the youngest to the ancient.'6 But cloth traders were frustrated by a lack of anywhere decent to buy and sell their wares, often resorting to selling their bolts of fabric on trestles laid out along the town's roads.

Much of the money for the new cloth hall came from the pockets of the merchants themselves, who were keen to have a central place where buyers and sellers could meet and trade during fixed hours, away from the dirt and undesirables of the open streets. The opening ceremony was, by all accounts, a day to remember; a large crowd gathered to watch a grand procession of local clothiers, headed by a noisy marching band,

* A 'piece' was a length of cloth 30 yards (or 27.4 metres) long.

stride into the Hall, followed by a spectacular pyrotechnic display. With all the pomp Yorkshire money could muster, the fireworks consisted 'of a beautiful Egyptian Pyramid illumined with spiral wheels, globes and vertical wheels to be set on fire by a pigeon'.[7]

Halifax also had another claim to fame. The Halifax Gibbet was the only guillotine in England. Thought to have been installed during the sixteenth century, it was used to execute petty thieves on market days, especially those who stole woollen cloth. Even before the days of the Piece Hall, Halifax had become well known for producing a fabric known as 'kersey', a tough but inexpensive woollen cloth used for military uniforms. During its manufacture, the cloth would be hung outside to dry on frames. Unattended cloth was liable to get stolen and so punishments were designed to be punitively harsh. Again, Defoe has something to add from his Halifax visit:

I must not quit Hallifax, till I give you some account of the famous course of justice anciently executed here, to prevent the stealing of cloth. Modern accounts pretend to say, it was for all sorts of felons; but I am well assured, it was first erected purely, or at least principally, for such thieves as were apprehended stealing cloth from the tenters.[8]

Halifax's reputation for zero tolerance was well known. One poem, 'The Beggar's Litany' by John Taylor (1622), famously includes the line 'From Hell, Hull and Halifax, Good Lord deliver us' (Hull was also famous for its harsh law enforcers). The poem continues:

> At Halifax, the Law so sharpe doth deale,
> That whoso more than thirteen pence doth steale,
> They have a jyn [engine] that wondrous quicke and well
> Sends Thieves all headless unto Heav'n or Hell.

The last execution using the Halifax Gibbet took place on 17 April 1650. Two men, Anthony Mitchell and John Wilkinson, were found guilty of stealing sixteen yards (14.6 metres) of russet-coloured kersey from tenterframes, along with two horses – a haul worth a total of £5.8s (about £1,000 in today's money). Traditionally, cloth stealers were made to sit in the town's stocks until the day of their execution on the following Saturday, with the cloth draped around their shoulders to add to their humiliation. Fortunately or unfortunately, depending on how you look at it, Mitchell and Wilkinson were found guilty on a Saturday and so were executed the same day.[9]

Back in the weavers' cottages, many of the people involved in the putting-out system were also part-time subsistence farmers, growing food for their families. The putting-out system suited merchants, as most of their labour-force was rural, cheap and outside the control of the urban guilds (who would try to protect wages, apprenticeships and quality control). But the system suited rural families as well, since it often allowed them to supplement other income streams, especially over the winter months, and to work from home with their children; it also gave them a degree of flexibility over the pattern of their working day.

As with all piecework carried out at home, however, the control lay ultimately with the merchant, who didn't have to bear the cost of renting the premises, training, lighting or heating. While some weavers owned their own looms, and saw themselves as independent artisans, others had to rent their machinery; and many a dispute arose when merchants refused to pay for finished cloth or collected more in loom rent than the weaving family had earned that week.

Lack of representation by any form of guild or labour union left outworkers especially vulnerable, but with few other options available to them wool workers made up the largest manufacturing sector in the British economy by the middle of the eighteenth century. Out of a population of around 6 million people, a quarter worked in wool textiles. Three dominant areas of production – the West Country, East Anglia and West Yorkshire – had already started to emerge, but, in the words of one historian, 'There was probably no county of England and Wales in which woollen cloth was not produced by the part-time work of peasants, farmers and agricultural labourers.'[10]

There were two broad categories of woollen cloth being

made in Britain at the time – broadcloth and worsted. Broad-cloth was made from short wool fibres, which were carded (using paddles that look a bit like dog brushes), spun and then woven on a wide loom. The cloth was then fulled, a process that involved scouring, followed by pounding, which created a bulkier, soft-felted fabric. These broadcloths were used for winter overcoats, blankets, uniforms – anything which needed to be warm and cosy.

Worsted cloth was made in a different way, using long-fibred wool, which would be combed (to encourage the fibres to lie parallel to each other), oiled, spun with a high level of twist and then woven into a lighter, finer, shinier fabric, perfect for men's suits, trousers and furnishing fabrics. Within both of these categories, there were dozens of variations and regional specialities with wonderful names – baize, serge, cheviot, melton, fearnought and petersham, to name but a handful.

By the end of the 1700s, the textile industry was beginning to change dramatically. Thomas Lombe's silk mill in Derby, built in 1721, is regarded as the world's first serious attempt at a mechanized textile factory and heralded a century of innovations that were to alter the face of the industry. Major innovations including John Kay's flying shuttle (1733), James Hargreaves' spinning jenny (1764), Richard Arkwright's water frame (1769) and Samuel Crompton's spinning mule (1779) revolutionized the way that both wool and cotton could be prepared, spun and woven. Many of the machines were too big or expensive for individual weaving families to purchase; some of the larger machines also needed water power to operate. The solution was to create purpose-built textile factories, large enough to house multiple machines, and situate them next to fast-flowing rivers, whose energy helped power large water wheels and provided convenient transport links. The locations of the mills, however, were often remote and the locally available workforce small in number.

The solution was a shocking one. Thrusting entrepreneurs, backed by government, were encouraged to recruit the most vulnerable people in society - orphans and destitute children - and turn them into what have been dubbed 'the white slaves of England'. There were plenty of precedents: between 1619 and 1622, 300 street children from London were sent to work in Virginia's tobacco plantations (where conditions were so harsh that only twelve of them were still alive in 1624[11]) and in 1630 the City of London had been asked to send over 'one hundred friendless boys and girls' to work in the new colony's spinning factories.

Between the 1650s and the 1680s, thousands of destitute, orphaned or imprisoned children are thought to have been spirited away by traffickers to work in America's newly emerging economy; more often than not poor children and teenagers were signed away by their own destitute families or tricked into signing themselves up as indentured servants who, when they arrived on faraway shores, were bought, sold and even gambled away. The captain of one ship, which regularly travelled between London and Jamaica, would 'visit the Clerkenwell House of Correction, ply with drink the girls who had been imprisoned there as disorderly, and "invite" them to go to the West Indies'.[12]

In 1796 Britain's then prime minister, William Pitt the Younger, gave a stirring speech to industrialists, promoting the benefits of child labour: 'experience has already shown, how much can be done by the industry of children. And the advantage of early employing them in such branches of manufacture as they were capable to execute'.[13] The parentless and abandoned were swept up into 'parish apprenticeships'; children as young as six were taken from the overflowing workhouses and orphanages in towns and cities, including London, and packed off to remote corners of the British countryside to work in the new textile mills. As one writer, born in 1823, recalled of his impoverished childhood:

> Very early in the last century there was an urgent need for children to work in the factories they were building then on all the streams they could find fit for their purpose in the West Riding of Yorkshire. The local supply of 'help' could not begin to meet the demand; and so the owners of the factories went or sent south to scour the asylums where children were to be found in swarms, to bring them north and set them to work as apprentices.[14]

Many of the children didn't know what they were going to or were duped with promises of a life of fresh air, plentiful food and an education. John Birley, an orphan living in Bethnal Green's workhouse, remembered:

> The same year my mother died, I being between six and seven years of age, there came a man looking for a number of parish apprentices. We were all ordered to come into the board room, about forty of us. There were, I dare say, about twenty gentlemen seated at a table, with pens and paper before them. Our names were called out one by one. We were all standing before them in a row. My name was called and I stepped out in the middle of the room. The man said, 'Well, John, you are a fine lad, would you like to go into the country?' We had often talked over amongst ourselves how we should like to be taken into the country. Mr. Nicholls the old master, used to tell us what fine sport we should have amongst the hills, what time we should have for play and pleasure. He said we should have plenty of roast beef and get plenty of money, and come back gentlemen to see our friends.[15]

In return for meagre food and board, children were expected to work fourteen to seventeen-hour days, six days a week, until they reached the age of twenty-one (or twenty-four, in some cases). John Birley worked from five in the morning until ten at night, ate two of his three small rations standing up at the machinery, and at night was locked in a room with the rest of the boys, three to a bed. Needless to say, dreams of 'roast beef and plenty of money' were hopelessly crushed: 'Mr. Needham, the master, had five sons: Frank, Charles, Samuel, Robert and John. The sons and a man named Swann, the overlooker, used to go up and down the mill with hazzle sticks. Frank once beat me till he frightened himself. He thought he had killed me.'[16]

As social historian and child labour expert Professor Jane Humphries notes, these were the 'real life Oliver Twists, left to the mercy of the parishes; their employment was nothing less than state-sponsored slavery [...] work became a substitute for social welfare'.[17] Employing children made financial sense; factory owners and overseers didn't want to employ adults, who would demand higher wages and less regimented ways of working. Children could be moulded and coerced. Not only that, but many of the machines were deliberately designed to be operated by young children, with their tiny hands, slight bodies and quick reflexes.

Children were often 'piecers' or 'pieceners' (mending broken threads), bobbin threaders or scavengers who crawled beneath the machinery and cleaned it. Alongside the regular beatings from overseers, growth-stunting work and noxious fibre frag-ments clogging up tiny lungs, accidents were commonplace, especially as tiredness set in. One child worker, John Allet, who was interviewed by the House of Commons Committee in 1832, recalled, 'I was an eye-witness of one. A child was working wool, that is, to prepare the wool for the machine; but the strap caught him, as he was hardly awake, and it carried him into the machinery; and we found one limb in one place, one in another, and he was cut to bits; his whole body went in, and was mangled.'[18]

Another boy, Joseph Hebergam, interviewed at the same time, described how he had started working fourteen-and-a-half-hour days at the age of seven and that the work had left his legs permanently deformed: 'in the morning I could scarcely walk, and my brother and sister used, out of kindness, to take me under each arm, and run with me to the mill, and my legs dragged on the ground; in consequence of the pain I could not walk.'[19]

Heartbreaking testimony after heartbreaking testimony reveals small voices from the mills that churned out wool and cotton for a hungry market. And while 'parish apprentices' filled the labour gap for the first few decades of textile mechanization, children from poor families out in the community soon found themselves also being sent to the deafening mills. Children had always been employed, of course, in a variety of capacities. For centuries, sons and daughters had been expected to help with housework, agricultural chores and, if possible, find paid work out of the house. In the words of one historian, 'child labour had a very long taproot in Britain'.[20] The difference now, thanks to the wool and cotton industries, was the scale on which they were put to work. The pre-industrial economy, especially in rural areas, wasn't really set up to give families the opportunity to regularly and consistently earn money from their children. But that all changed with the coming of an era of mass-manufactured textiles, when 'Early industrial Britain was a booming economy with an insatiable appetite for strong backs and nimble fingers.'[21]

Although many saw child labour as a natural part of the working-class experience, not everyone condoned it. Some of the most probing and influential works of Georgian and Victorian literature focused on the topic of child labour. Spurred on by parliamentary enquiries into the conditions at textiles mills, mines and other factories, authors such as Elizabeth Barrett Browning, Charles Kingsley, Elizabeth Gaskell, and, perhaps most famously, Charles Dickens, took up the plight of society's most vulnerable; *David Copperfield* – Dickens's eighth novel, published in 1850 – is based, in part, on Dickens's own experiences of working in a boot-blacking factory at the age of twelve. These, and other works, exposed the middle-class reader to the horrors of child labour and gave traction to the few campaigners who were fighting for reform.

Change was slow, frustrated in part by the many members of Parliament and society who had interests in cloth manufacture. Some voiced their concerns that, if children didn't work, their fate would be even worse. The Irish writer William

Cooke Taylor, an opponent of anti-child labour legislation, insisted:

Persons enter a mill [...] they see the figures of the little piecers and cleaners employed in their monotonous routine, [...] and they think how much more delightful would have been the gambol of free limbs on the hill-side, the inhaling of the fresh breeze, the sight of the green mead with its spangles of buttercups and daisies, the song of the bird, and the humming of the bee! But they should compare the aspect of the youthful operatives with other sights which they must have met in the course of their experience, as we too often have in ours: we have seen children perishing from sheer hunger in the mud-hovel, or in the ditch by the wayside.[22]

Others simply failed to believe there was a problem; Andrew Ure, a Scottish doctor who was a passionate supporter of the factory system, penned this astonishing description in the first half of the nineteenth century:

I have visited many factories, both in Manchester and in the surrounding districts, during a period of several months, entering the spinning rooms [...] and I never saw a single instance of corporal chastisement inflicted on a child, nor indeed did I ever see children in ill-humour.

They seemed to be always cheerful and alert, taking pleasure in the light play of their muscles, enjoying the mobility natural to their age. The scene of industry, so far from exciting sad emotions in my mind, was always exhilarating. It was delightful to observe the nimbleness with which they pieced the broken ends, as the mule-carriage began to recede from the fixed roller-beam, and to see them at leisure, after a few seconds' exercise of their tiny fingers, to amuse themselves in any attitude they chose, till the stretch and winding-on were once more completed. The work of these lively elves seemed to resemble a sport, in which habit gave them a pleasing dexterity.[23]

While Dr Ure saw 'lively elves', others thankfully didn't and the campaign against child labour resulted in the first of many Acts designed to limit children's working hours. The Factory Act of 1833 banned children under nine from working in textiles and limited the hours for those aged between nine and thirteen, although in reality enforcement was difficult. Nearly thirty years after the Factory Act, half of all of England's children between the ages of five and fifteen were still classed as 'working'.

Across the water in American mills, change was also piece-meal. Opponents of child labour tried to pass various pieces of legislation during the late nineteenth and early twentieth centuries but often came up against opposition. Most business, church and government organizations were fervently anti-regulation, preferring instead to let individual states and mill owners set their own voluntary agreements. The pro-child labour movement also had plenty of advocates who insisted that life in the mill was not only benign for children, but actively positive: 'that to most of these unfortunate people, factory life is a distinct improvement over the log cabin, salt pork, and peach brandy, white-trash and Georgia-cracker type of life from which many of them were sifted out when the mills came.'[24] It wasn't until the passing of the Fair Labor Standards Act of 1938 that US law made it illegal for children under sixteen to work in manufacturing or mining.

It's almost impossible to imagine the pace of change in the woollen industry during the nineteenth century in particular. At the start of the century, there were around 250,000 hand-loom weavers across Britain. By 1850 it had fallen to 40,000 and by 1860, only 3,000 remained.[25] A well-known folk song called 'The Weaver and the Factory Maid' (collected by A. L. Lloyd and others), captures the shift from home-based hand-weaving to factory work:

Where are the girls I'll tell you plain
The girls have gone to weave by steam
And if you'd find them you must rise at dawn
And trudge to the mill in the early morn.

To state that the wool and cotton industries detonated one way of life and replaced it with another is no exaggeration; their influence cannot be overstated. When textile mills moved from water power to steam power, it transformed coal mining into a major industry; wherever coal was plentiful, such as West Yorkshire, mills would spring up close by and workers would flood to them in their thousands. The machines that clattered in textile mills boosted the iron industry. The demand for quick, efficient methods of bringing raw materials to the textile mills and taking away the finished cloth stimulated first the canal system and then the growth of the railways. At the beginning of nineteenth century, the population of Great Britain was just over 9 million people. Only fifty years later, it was nearly 16 million.

Perhaps no other place embodies this explosion in population and industry more than Bradford. At the end of the 1700s Bradford was just a small rural market town, nestling at the foothills of the Pennines. It had a population of around 13,000 people and one woollen mill, making worsted fabric. By 1850, the population had swollen to over 100,000, with 129 mills. Twenty-five years later, the population had nearly doubled again and by the end of the century 350 woollen mills dominated the skyline, churning out two-thirds of Britain's *entire* wool production – Bradford had become the textile capital of the world.

It was a place uniquely suited to factory-based wool

production. Bradford had everything going for it: plentiful local supplies of coal and iron ore to make and feed the machinery; quarries with sandstone to construct the factories and housing; soft water (for cleaning the wool) piped from nearby dales; a canal that linked it to ports and international markets and, by the middle of the 1840s, a railway. Workers came from all over the country and further beyond, especially Ireland and Germany, hoping to find a job in the wool trade – by the middle of the 1850s, it is estimated that half the workforce had been born outside the city boundaries.

The wealth generated by the wool industry turned Bradford into a prosperous, architectural gem of a city. Success attracted success. There was clearly money to be made. The *Bradford Observer* noted in 1836, 'The manufacturers are removing to Bradford as fast as they can get accommodated with looms.' But what a city of contrasts – while splendid new civic buildings expressed the confidence of a city dubbed 'Worstedopolis' and wealthy families enjoyed the comfort of large villas and elegant townhouses, only streets away most of the factory workers endured overcrowded back-to-backs and slum housing. James Burnley, who wrote for the *Bradford Observer*, commented, 'I wonder how many of the well-dressed, well-fed people, who daily pass up and down Westgate, have really any experience of, or seriously consider, the wretchedness, the misery and the disease, of which the entrance to Silsbridge Lane is the threshold.'[26]

In 1843, one health commissioner declared Bradford to be the 'dirtiest, filthiest, worst regulated town in the kingdom' while Georg Weerth, a radical German pamphleteer and good friend of Karl Marx, famously wrote in 1846, 'Every other factory town in England is a paradise in comparison to this hole [...] in Bradford, however, you think you have been lodged with the devil incarnate. If anyone wants to feel how a poor sinner is tormented in purgatory, let him travel to Bradford.'

Things were bad, even by the standards of the day – average life expectancy among textile workers was just eighteen years of age. Workers and their families had to contend with a multitude of assaults on their health, some more surprising than others. Along with the usual suspects, caused by over-crowding, open sewers and polluted drinking water, working with wool rendered them vulnerable to other diseases. The people who sorted the wool bales when they arrived in the mill seemed to be succumbing to something that became known as the 'woolsorters' disease', or '*la maladie de Bradford*'. What started as little more than a cough or tightness in the chest ended, only days later, with a visit from the undertaker. It took until the end of the nineteenth century and the work of Dr Friederich Eurich – whose father, ironically, was a textile merchant who had brought the family over from Germany to Bradford – to figure out that 'the dark figure on the ware-house stairs'[27] was in fact anthrax, brought in with sacks of imported wool.

Anthrax and sheep also hold a special place in the history of medicine. As a disease, it has a significant pedigree – many scholars believe that one of the ten plagues of Egypt, as told in the story of Exodus, was probably anthrax. In the founding myth of the Israelites, God brings 'a terrible plague on your livestock in the field – on your horses and donkeys and camels and on your cattle and sheep and goats'. By the nineteenth century, anthrax was rife, especially among sheep and cattle – in France alone, 10 per cent of all sheep died from the disease each year. Knowing that anthrax seemed to affect sheep in particular, the French chemist Louis Pasteur decided to perform his most audacious experiment to date.

Most scientists were convinced that anthrax was caused either by spontaneous generation or by sheep being exposed to some outside factor, such as hot weather or toxic plants. Pasteur, however, was convinced that microbes were to blame. In May 1881, in front of an excited public audience, he gathered together fifty sheep. Twenty-five of the sheep he injected with an anthrax vaccine he'd been working on. The other twenty-five – the control group – got nothing. A month after the vaccine, both groups were deliberately infected with anthrax. Two days after reinfection, the crowd reassembled to see the results. All the sheep who'd been vaccinated were alive and well. Of the control group, all but three sickly-looking sheep had already expired. By the end of the day, the last three were also dead.

The demonstration was a resounding success. Between 1882 and 1893, nearly 4 million French cows and sheep received the anthrax vaccine. The number of livestock dying from the disease plummeted and the use of Pasteur's vaccine quickly spread to neighbouring countries and beyond. Thanks to sheep, a simple experiment and Pasteur's dogged research, which built on earlier work by the German microbiologist Robert Koch, scientific notions we now hold as truths – such as germ theory and the effectiveness of vaccination – became mainstream. It was just one of many occasions – as we'll see in the next chapter – when sheep and science made history.

14

UP, UP AND AWAY

Bad science, sex and sheep in space

In 1757 the first edition of a very unusual guidebook came out. It was called *Harris's List of Covent Garden Ladies*. This little black book contained the names, addresses, prices and 'bedroom specialities' of central London's prostitutes, including details of each woman's likes, hobbies, life history and looks. For wealthy men in the eighteenth century, whether far from home or simply seeking the thrill of illicit sex, prostitutes were a cheap diversion. And, while there were few qualms about picking out a lady from Harris's list, one thought would have been at the forefront of any Georgian gentleman's mind: the spectre of a sexually transmitted disease.

Sheep intestines have been used as condoms for millennia; some of the first early adopters of ovine contraception were Roman soldiers, who covered their penises with dried, stretched pieces of gut, kept in place with a bit of string. By the 1700s, however, the art of fashioning male contraception from unwanted offal had reached a level of sophistication few could have imagined. Small-scale manufacturers, working out of the big cities of Europe, had a ready supply of sheep guts from local butchers and abattoirs. The intestines were first soaked and washed in lye, and then scraped smooth with a knife. These were then exposed to sulphuric steam, which softened the tissue, and then rewashed in lye, soap and water.

The crudest condoms were just a square of intestine made into a small drawstring bag, which fitted loosely over the man's 'yard' and tied with a jaunty ribbon. English manufacturers soon experimented with other, more tailored models, with seductive French names such as *baudruches* and *superfines* designed to tickle the imagination and add a little continental *je ne sais quoi*. These new condoms were shaped over glass penis-shaped moulds of different sizes, making them a snugger fit, and, if your budget stretched far enough, you could even ask for the super-secure *double* (one condom fitted inside another for extra protection) or the scented condom, perfumed 'for her pleasure' with essential oils and spices.[1] The latter, no doubt, offered a welcome relief from the inevitable pong of unwashed bodies and warm sheep gut.

At the end of the 1990s, archaeologists had the rather unusual privilege of being allowed to sift through the remains of a seventeenth-century toilet at Dudley Castle in the West Midlands. The toilet had been used by 300 Royalist soldiers who had been garrisoned and then besieged in the castle during the English Civil War. In the process of working their way through 100 cubic feet of human excrement and other waste, the archaeologists discovered the oldest condom found anywhere in the world – a reusable sheep-gut dating back to the 1640s.

The English Birth Rate Commission, in 1666, first uses the word 'condom' – initially spelled 'condon' – hailing it as the reason for a significant fall in the country's birth rate. Most men, however, weren't using condoms for family planning, but rather to protect themselves from the horror of syphilis, a disease that had been romping its way through Europe since the late 1400s. The word 'syphilis', incidentally, also has a sheepy connection; in 1530 the Italian physician and poet Girolamo Fracastoro wrote a pastoral poem which featured a shepherd boy, Syphilus, who is struck down with the terrible disease by the Greek god Apollo, as a punishment for insulting him. The name stuck.

Soldiers and sailors were particularly good at spreading syphilis, often by sleeping with local prostitutes. As the disease seemed to spread from contact with foreigners, nations blamed each other – the English called it the 'French Disease', the Italians called it the 'Turkish Disease', the French called it the 'Italian Disease' and so on. People were horrified by its ghastly, disfiguring effects, which are vividly described by the historian Jared Diamond: 'Its pustules often covered the body from the head to the knees, caused flesh to fall off people's faces, and led to death within a few months.'[2]

Sheep-gut condoms were the only reliable protection

against what was, at that time, a deadly, incurable condition. Brothels sold them to clients and even the world's greatest lover, Casanova, became a convert. At first, the unstoppable lothario had expressed his dislike for what he called 'dead animal skin',[3] but soon came around after he realized how effective they were at protecting him from disease. He became adept at testing condoms for leaks by blowing them up with his mouth and wrote, at length, about trying to get partners to get onboard the notion of what he called a 'prophylactic against anxiety'. Two hundred years later, in 1988, the UK's Health Education Authority brought out a now-iconic poster, promoting condoms for use against HIV. The poster featured an array of historic condoms (including one used by Casanova), accompanied by the words: 'So if the world's greatest lover made do with sheep gut, surely you can use a condom.'

Thinking on the notion of blowing up condoms, before Michael Faraday invented the first rubber balloon in 1824, toy balloons and footballs were made from – among other things – sheep offal. Bladders, inflated and then dried, created excellent, lightweight balls, while intestines made sausage-shaped balloons not dissimilar to those used by modellers or 'twisters' today. Children's parties must have been a hoot. It was also a balloon – on a much bigger scale – that made sheep history on 19 September 1783.

The previous June, brothers Jacques-Etienne and Joseph-Michel Montgolfier had successfully demonstrated the first ever hot-air balloon flight. The balloon, made from fabric and paper, and lit from underneath by a straw fire, was unmanned but managed a respectable ten-minute flight before floating back down to earth. King Louis XVI, hearing of the brothers' success, ordered the brothers to bring their invention to Paris and test it in front of the royal palace at Versailles.

The king also wanted to see what would happen if you put a human inside the balloon and suggested the brothers tested it using two criminals pulled from the king's prison. The brothers gracefully declined the offer of convict guinea-pigs and suggested instead that they first send a sheep (called Montauciel, meaning 'reach the sky'), a duck and a cockerel along for the ride. Far from being random test pilots, the brothers thought the combination of animals would provide an interesting experiment – the sheep's physiology was thought to be close match for the human body and the duck was chosen as a control as it was used to flying at high altitudes. The cockerel posed an interesting scientific conundrum – what would happen to a bird that wasn't used to flying at high altitudes?

The farmyard flight-crew lifted off, nearly 1,600 feet (500 metres) into the air, watched by an open-mouthed crowd of 130,000 people, the king and Marie Antoinette. After a heart-stopping eight-minute, two-mile (3.2-kilometre) flight the balloon drifted back down with a surprisingly gentle landing. All three passengers were alive. The sheep, duck and cockerel were crowned 'heroes of the air' and, so the legend goes, sent to live out the rest of their days in Louis's Royal Menagerie. Just two months later, Jean-François Pilâtre de Rozier and François Laurent le Vieux d'Arlandes made the first human trip in a balloon. Thanks to plucky Montauciel and her fowl friends, people could at last leave the surface of the earth and soar to the heavens. The wait for human flight was finally over.

The ordeal for sheep, however, wasn't. Now the art of ballooning had been perfected, the next question was how to come back down to earth. Early parachute experiments often involved dropping animals, wearing prototype parachutes, from hot-air balloons. In 1817, Mr Renault from New Orleans attempted to drop a sheep from his hot-air balloon, 'by means of a parachute'.[4] No records exist of whether the sheep wafted down safely, although judging by most other parachute tests of the day, things probably didn't go well. Only a few years earlier a British army officer, Colonel Thornton, had dropped his dog, who was wearing a parachute, from a hot-air balloon in London. According to contemporary sources, the unfortunate canine 'descended to earth with great velocity' before hitting the ground with a crunch.[5] Remarkably, despite sustaining a number of injuries, the dog survived.

The Montgolfier brothers weren't far off in their assertion that sheep had a similar physiology to humans. Sheep are bright, social creatures whose large body size, long life and docile nature have made them an attractive testing ground for scientists through the ages. In 1667, for example, the French physician Jean-Baptiste Denys performed the first fully documented human blood transfusion using lamb's blood. The patient was a sickly fifteen-year-old boy who had been suffering from blood loss, thanks to overzealous leech-use by a previous doctor. Denys managed to get about 12 fluid ounces (341 ml) of lamb's blood into the boy and, miraculously, he lived.

Emboldened, Denys repeated the experiment on a labourer, who also survived the procedure. We now know that human-animal transfusions are deadly – Denys' two patients probably survived only because of the small amounts of blood involved – but he wasn't so lucky with his third patient, a madman called Antoine Mauroy, who died during his third transfusion. Denys was accused of murder by Mauroy's wife and, although eventually acquitted, was put off practising medicine for the rest of his life. It wasn't until 1902, and Karl Landsteiner's groundbreaking discovery of the four different blood groups and their incompatibility, that blood transfusions became a safe and common hospital procedure.

Sheep have been at the centre of some historic scientific and medical breakthroughs, from womb transplants to growing new heart valves, but the most famous is, of course, Dolly the Sheep. Dolly was the first mammal to be cloned from an adult cell. In 1996, scientists at the Roslin Institute, Scotland, used cells from the mammary gland of a six-year-old Finnish Dorset sheep to create Dolly. The experiment proved that specialized cells could be used to create an exact copy of the sheep they came from. In fact, Dolly wasn't the first ever cloned animal – that honour goes to Megan and Morag, two sheep that had been cloned from embryonic cells at Roslin a year earlier. Dolly went on to live to the age of six and a half, gave birth to six healthy, non-clone lambs, and after her death her body was donated to the National Museum of Scotland in Edinburgh, where she has become the star attraction.

A less well known, but equally gripping, scientific break-through, also has sheep at the centre of its story. In 1958 a man with a strong Eastern European accent strolled into the animal sciences department at the University of Sydney. He announced himself to be Dr Steven Salamon and explained that he knew how to artificially breed livestock, a scientific skill yet to be cracked by the West. Would the department, he asked, give him a job?

As a young man, Salamon had served in the Hungarian army and fought alongside the Germans in the Second World War, but at the end of the war he was captured by the Soviets and sent to a prison camp in Siberia. There he stayed for three hellish years, narrowly surviving death. At one point, Salamon had been thrown into a frozen pit by the guards but managed to survive by covering himself with the dead bodies and clothes of other people who had suffered the same fate.

After the war, Salamon qualified as an animal scientist, but he wanted to live somewhere as far removed from the icy gulag as possible and came to Australia. From the early 1960s Salamon led experiments in artificial insemination in sheep flocks and developing methods of freezing and storing semen. His groundbreaking work not only changed the face of modern sheep farming but ultimately inspired research into human IVF.

After his death in 2017, at the ripe old age of ninety-eight, his former colleagues decided to defrost some of the ram semen Dr Salamon had frozen back in 1968. The sperm was now the best part of fifty years old and surely far too long in the freezer to still be useful. The semen was inserted into Merino ewes and, to everyone's astonishment, the sheep not only got pregnant, but the quality of the frozen sperm was as good as the day it was first produced. This half-century-old sperm set the world record for the oldest semen ever to be used but, more importantly, showed scientists the potential for long-term conservation of genetic material. The ramifications were profound – from freezing eggs and sperm of patients undergoing long treatment to the preservation of endangered animals, Dr Salamon's work changed our expectations of what is possible in genetic science. As one Australian journalist noted, drily, a legacy 'very apt for a man who himself came out of the freezer'.[6]

The more we find out about sheep, however, the more complex the questions that arise surrounding animal experiments.

For thousands of years, sheep have been stereotyped as stupid, unthinking creatures. We couldn't have got it more wrong. One study, in 2001, showed that sheep can recognize and remember at least fifty different faces. What's more, they can still recognize these same faces after two years. Humans have a specialized neural mechanism for visual recognition, which allows us to differentiate and recall lots of different faces. This is thought to be one of the most important traits needed for social interaction and relationships – imagine a world where everyone you met was a stranger. It turns out that sheep have similar neural systems in their temporal and frontal lobes and can recognize both humans and other sheep by their faces, even after long periods apart. What's even more incredible is that the same experiment showed that sheep can distinguish between different facial expressions and, as with humans, prefer a smile to a sad face.[7]

Another study, in Australia, looked at how sheep dealt with trying to find their way through a complex maze. The experiment showed that not only did the sheep navigate their way through without too many problems but that on every subsequent occasion they got faster and faster. What took two minutes on the first day, took only thirty seconds by the third. And, even more astonishing, six weeks later when they were tested again the sheep remembered their way through and equalled their previous best times.[8]

Sometimes fact is stranger than fiction. Back in 2004, the

inhabitants of a Pennine hill village were flummoxed; how were the sheep that grazed on the edge of the village of Marsden getting over a cattle grid to ravage the lawns of local residents? The cattle grids had been installed years ago to keep the sheep on the moorland, but lately they seemed to have taken a fancy to the village's flower beds and front gardens. The grids were too wide to leap and too tricky to tiptoe across, so how were the sheep crossing? Villagers were amazed to discover that the sheep were getting on their backs and rolling across the cattle grids, like SAS commandos. Scientists who work with sheep weren't surprised, however. One neuroscientist at the University of Cambridge found that sheep performed at a level similar to monkeys and humans in certain learning tasks. In a recent interview Professor Jenny Morton explained just how talented sheep are: 'They've got big brains - I'd challenge someone who wasn't an expert to tell the difference between a monkey brain and a sheep brain. And they are immensely trainable. You can take any old sheep out of a field and in two weeks teach it to do a task it might take a monkey nine months to learn.'[9]

One of the most interesting recent discoveries, however, is that sheep can be gay. In any flock of domesticated sheep, about 8 per cent of the males seem to prefer the company of other males, even in the presence of fertile females.[10] There are plenty of other examples of homosexuality in the natural world. From female macaques to male fruit flies, many species engage in same-sex behaviour, whether by accident or for pleasure and social bonding. The difference has always been, however, that animals in nature seem to switch between homosexual and heterosexual behaviour; they don't show consistent sexual orientation. Only two species have ever been seen to show same-sex preference for life, even when partners of the opposite sex are readily available. One is humans and the other is, surprisingly, domesticated sheep.

For a long time, homosexual behaviour was seen as 'unnatural'. On the face of it, it doesn't seem beneficial for the survival of the human species to have same-sex couples, who won't be able to pass on their genes to the next generation. And yet what the science of sheep sexuality shows us is that homosexual behaviour doesn't challenge Darwinian ideas but may in fact reinforce them.

One idea is that there may be one particular gene that expresses itself in different ways. The same gene that expresses itself as homosexual behaviour in male sheep might be the same gene that increases a female sheep's fertility. The female siblings of gay sheep produce more offspring than average, helping that specific gene to carry on in subsequent generations. In other words, the gene that predisposes some sheep to be homosexual promotes reproductive success in others. Sheep farmers have, over the centuries, enhanced the effects of this gene by choosing and breeding from females that are the most fertile.

———

So what's the future for sheep? We're at a crossroads. While in the West, many people are eschewing sheep meat for health and ecological reasons, demand from the developing world is predicted to soar over the next few decades. On one hand, we have a romantic view of sheep farming – the lonely shepherd, herding his or her flock on upland farms and maintaining an ancient and important way of life. On the other, we have vast, intensive agri-business, churning out meat and wool on an industrial scale, to feed consumer demand for cheap meat and affordable textiles. Throw in issues such as animal welfare, the health implications of red meat, climate change and bio-diversity loss, and you have a situation for sheep farming that's full of contradictions and dilemmas.

The future for sheep is uncertain. The planet cannot tolerate a future of overstocking and aggressively intensive farming practices that pay scant attention to the animals' welfare. Soil degradation, water pollution, carbon emissions, deforestation and other environmental headaches are already upon us. The global livestock industry has degraded land, contributed to the greenhouse effect, polluted watercourses and had a disastrous effect on biodiversity. And, if we look at the entire production cycle of sheep farming (either for wool or meat) we see that, at every stage of the process, issues arise. Whether it's emissions generated by fertilizer and animal feeds, what to do with endless piles of manure, chopping down trees for pastureland, methane from sheep's digestion, or the carbon cost of transporting sheep and animal feed by vehicle – on the face of it, sheep don't look like a sustainable option.

And yet we mustn't throw the baby out with the bathwater. Current methods of intensive vegetable and crop production are hardly an improvement. As the demand for plant-based foods and vegetable fats increases, it is producing equally destructive environmental effects in many parts of the world – deforestation of rainforests for palm oil, soil degradation, vast use of pesticides and fungicides. Added to this, there are significant concerns surrounding genetically modified soybean cultivation. In the UK, where the pulling up of hedgerows to make large, monocultural fields has long been a cause of environmental anxiety, intensive arable farming has decimated pollinator numbers and led to a dramatic decline in wild plant species.

It's an interesting time for sheep farming, not least because we'll have to pick our way through different points of view. The solutions will also be highly localized and nuanced. Organizations such as the Sustainable Food Trust and the UN Intergovernmental Panel on Climate Change believe that sheep can, if managed properly, be part of the solution. Soil degradation, for example, could be reversed if we return to mixed farming systems which include plenty of pasture and nitrogen-fixing legumes grazed by sheep and cattle.

Pastureland – especially if it is sown with long-rooted varieties of grass – also captures and locks away carbon. In some instances, grazing can actually improve biodiversity; in the UK, many of our different landscapes – heathland, coastal marshes, wood pasture and grassland – all rely on a bit of grazing to maintain the variety of plants and wildlife that live there. For some areas, such as upland, animal grazing is often the only economically viable and productive use of land – crops simply won't grow there.

There's also the cultural legacy. For thousands of years, people have lived with, looked after and built their environments around sheep. Many of the rural traditions and skills that we value in the UK, for example, come from sheep farming and wool production. From dry-stone walls to agricultural shows, sheepdog trials to spinning and weaving, the heritage and landscape that we cherish, and still enjoy, comes in large part from centuries of sheep farming. Like ancient crafts or period buildings, traditional farming allows us to keep a link to our past and helps us understand who we are. We've got to be so careful not to let agriculture become something so technologically efficient and mechanized that we lose touch with the fact that we are dealing with other living creatures and plants. It's heartening to see how many people are re-engaging with the countryside, whether by visiting country shows, reading rural-interest magazines or watching nature programmes on TV. We must somehow, however, join up this deep affection we have for a rural way of life with the choices we make as consumers and the agricultural policies we support at a national level. Our landscape, our wildlife, our towns and villages, our history, our language and our sense of identity all come, in no small part, from the thousands of years we have shared the planet with ewes, lambs and rams.

Sheep have changed us as much as we have changed them.

NOTES

Chapter One: How to Get a Sheep to Stand Still

1   Abell, J. T. *el al.*, 'Urine salts elucidate Early Neolithic animal management at Aşıklı Höyük, Turkey,' in *Science Advances*, Vol. 5, No. 4 (2019).

2   University of Cambridge, 'Was the fox prehistoric man's best friend?' (31 Jan. 2011). See www.cam.ac.uk/research/news/was-the-fox-prehistoric-mans-best-friend

3   Tomalin, Claire, *The Life and Death of Mary Wollstonecraft*, Penguin (2012).

4   Sample, Ian, 'Why is a woman breastfeeding a tiger?', *The Guardian* (7 Apr. 2005).

5   Diamond, Jared, *Guns, Germs, and Steel: The Fates of Human Societies*, W.W. Norton & Company (1997).

6   Cornell University, 'Silver fox study reveals genetic clues to social behavior', ScienceDaily (27 Sept. 2018). See www.sciencedaily.com/releases/2018/09/180927105659.htm

7   'Hints of 7,200-Year-Old Cheese Create a Scientific Stink', *National Geographic* (6 Sept. 2018). See www.nationalgeographic.co.uk/history-and-civilisation/2018/09/hints-7200-year-old-cheese-create-scientific-stink

8   Becker, Cornelia, *et al.*, 'The Textile Revolution. Research into the Origin and Spread of Wool Production between the Near East and Central Europe', in *Journal for Ancient Studies*, Special Volume (2016), edited by Gerd Graßhoff and Michael Meyer.

9 Gleba, Margarita, 'Sheep to Textiles: Approaches to Investigating Ancient Wool Trade' (2014). See www.repository.cam.ac.uk/handle/1810/254046

10 Ryder, M. L., *Sheep and Man*, Gerald Duckworth and Co. Ltd (1983), p. 96.

Chapter Two: Wool's Scaly Secret

1 'Ice Mummies: Siberian Ice Maiden' PBS Airdate: 24 Nov. 1998 A BBC/Horizon NOVA/WGBH Co-production © 1997 BBC © 1998 WGBH Educational Foundation.

2 Laufer, Berthold, 'The Early History of Felt', in *American Anthropologist*, Vol. 32, No. 1 (Jan.-Mar. 1930).

3 Robertson, William, *A Dictionary of Latin Phrases: Comprehending a Methodical Digest of the Various Phrases*, printed by A. J. Valpy for Baldwin, Cradock and Joy (1824).

4 Blakolmer, Fritz, 'A "Special Procession" in Minoan Seal Images: Observations on Ritual Dress in Minoan Crete' in: P. Pavúk et al. (eds), EUDAIMON. Studies in Honour of Prof. Jan Bouzek, Conference, Prague (Prag-Brno 2018), 29-50.

5 Herodotus, *The Persian Wars* (Book IV), from *The Greek Historians*, edited by Francis R. B. Godolphin (Copyright 1942, renewed 1970 by Random House, Inc.).

6 Laufer, Berthold, 'The Early History of Felt', in *American Anthropologist*, Vol. 32, No. 1 (Jan.-Mar. 1930).

7 Zerjal, Tatiana *et al.*, 'The Genetic Legacy of the Mongols', in *The American Journal of Genetics*, Vol. 72, No. 3 (2003).

Chapter Three: Why Some Sheep are So Rooed

1 Barber, E. J. W., *Prehistoric Textiles: The Development of Cloth in the Neolithic and Bronze Ages, with Special Reference to the Aegean*, Princeton University Press (1992).

2 Barket, Theresa M., and Bell, Colleen, 'Tabular Scrapers: Function Revisited' in *Near Eastern Archaeology*, Vol. 74, No. 1 (2011).

3 Ryder, M. L., 'The Interaction Between Biological and Technological Change During the Development of Different Fleece Types in Sheep', in *Anthropozoologica*, Vol. 16 (1992).

4 Milleker, Elizabeth J., *The Year One: Art of the Ancient World East and West*, The Metropolitan Museum of Art (2000).

5 Okrostsvaridze. A. et al. 'A modern field investigation of the mythical "gold sands" of the ancient Colchis Kingdom and "Golden Fleece" phenomena', in *Quaternary International*, Vol. 409, Part A (2016).

6 Varro, M. T., from 'The Husbandry of Livestock', in *De Re Rustica* II, *Delphi Complete Works of Varro* (Illustrated), Delphi Classics (2017).

7 Kissell, Mary Lois, 'Ancient Greek Yarn-Making' in *The Metropolitan Museum of Art Bulletin*, Vol. 13 (1918).

8 Quick, Graeme R., *Remarkable Australian Farm Machines: Ingenuity on the Land*, Rosenberg (2007), p. 145.

9 Ibid., p. 145.

Chapter Four: Tough as Old Boots

1 Strabo, *The Geography of Strabo*, Book IV, Chapter 4, published in Vol. II of the Loeb Classical Library edition (1923).

2 Kropff, Antony, *New English translation of the Price Edict of Diocletianus* (2016). See www.academia.edu/23644199/New_English_translation_of_the_Price_Edict_of_Diocletianus

3 Green, Miranda, *Animals in Celtic Life and Myth*, Routledge (1998), p. 31.

4 Strabo, *The Geography of Strabo*, Book IV, Chapter 4, published in Vol. II of the Loeb Classical Library edition (1923).

5 Cornell University, 'Lactose Intolerance Linked To Ancestral Environment.' ScienceDaily (2 Jun. 2005). See www.sciencedaily.com/releases/2005/06/050602012109.htm

6 Columella, *De Re Rustica* VII. 2.1, and Varro, *Res Rusticae* 2.11.1–3.

7 Balthazar, C. F. *et al.*, 'Sheep's milk: Physicochemical Characteristics and Relevance for Functional Food Development', in *Comprehensive Reviews in Food Science and Food Safety*, Vol. 16, No. 2 (2017).

8 Pliny the Elder, *The Natural History*, Chap. 97, 'Various Kinds of Cheese', translated by John Bostock, M.D., F.R.S., H.T. Riley, Esq., B.A. London. Taylor and Francis, Red Lion Court, Fleet Street (1855).

9   Homer, *The Odyssey*, translated by Samuel Butler, Longmans (1898).

10   Green, Miranda, *Animals in Celtic Life and Myth*, Routledge (1998), p. 124.

11   Merrifield, Ralph, *The Archaeology of Ritual and Magic*, Batsford (1987), p. 51.

12   Keys, David, 'The boneyard of the bizarre that rewrites our Celtic past to include hybrid-animal monster myths', *Independent* (11 Jul. 2015). See www.independent.co.uk/news/science/archaeology/news/the-boneyard-of-the-bizarre-that-rewrites-our-celtic-past-to-include-hybrid-animal-monster-myths-10381965.html

13   Gosset, A. L. J., *Shepherds of Britain: Scenes from Shepherd Life Past and Present*, Read Country Books Ltd (2017).

14   Tacitus, Cornelius, 'Germania' XII in *Agricola and Germania*, edited by James Rives and translated by Harold Mattingly, Penguin Classics (2010).

15   Vanden Berghe, I. *et al.*, 'Towards the identification of dyestuffs in Early Iron Age Scandinavian peat bog textiles', in *Journal of Archaeological Science*, Vol. 36 (2009).

Chapter Five: Rhymes and Ridiculous Cures

1   Opie, Iona and Opie, Peter, *The Oxford Dictionary of Nursery Rhymes*, Oxford University Press (1997).

2   Burg, David F., *A World History of Tax Rebellions*, Routledge (2003), p. 95.

3   Cold Spring Harbor Laboratory, 'Scientists Identify Genetic Basis for the Black Sheep of the Family', ScienceDaily (11 Jul. 2008). See www.sciencedaily.com/releases/2008/07/080710174236.htm

4   Opie, Iona and Tatem, Moira, *Oxford Dictionary of Superstitions*, Oxford University Press (2009), p. 347.

5   Ibid., p. 348.

6   Ibid., p. 29.

7   Steele, John M., 'Astronomy and culture in Late Babylonian Uruk', in *Proceedings of the International Astronomical Union*, Vol. 7, No. S278 ('Oxford IX' International Symposium on Archaeoastronomy) (2011).

8   Camden, W., *Remains Concerning Britain*, reprinted by John Russell Smith (1870), p. 317.
9   Hoskins, W. G., *Provincial England: Essays in Social and Economic History*, Macmillan (1963), p. 4.
10 Ordnance Survey, 'Guide to Scots Origins of Place Names in Britain', http://media.scotslanguage.com/library/document/scots_guide.pdf
11 Redmond, Gabriel O'C. 'Origin of the Saying "By Hook or by Crook"', *The Journal of the Royal Historical and Archaeological Association of Ireland*, Fourth Series (1887).
12 Ray, J., *A Collection Of English Proverbs Digested Into A Convenient Method For The Speedy Finding Any One Upon Occasion; With Short Annotations*. Cambridge, Printed By John Hayes, Printer To The University, For W. Morden (1678).
13 Plutarch, *Septem Sapientium Convivium* Vol. II, Loeb Classical Library edition (1928).

Chapter Six: Mr and Mrs Bo-Peep

1   Ganesh, Gayatri and Ghotge, Nitya, 'Hidden and unaccounted for: understanding maternal health needs and practices of semi-nomadic shepherd women in Maharashtra, India', in *MIDIRS Midwifery Digest*, Vol. 27, No. 4 (2017).
2   Walton, C. L., 'Transhumance and its Survival in Great Britain', in *The Geographical Teacher*, Vol. 10, No. 3 (Autumn 1919).
3   Bowie, G. G. S., 'New Sheep for Old - Changes in Sheep Farming in Hampshire, 1792-1879', in *The Agricultural History Review*, Vol. 35, No. 1 (1987).
4   Gaskell, Elizabeth, *North and South*, (1855), reprinted by Wordsworth Classics (1993), p. 54.
5   Youatt, W., *Sheep; their breeds, management and diseases. To which is added, the mountain shepherd's manual*, Baldwin and Craddock (1837), p. 430.
6   Quoted in Buchanan Given, James, *Society and Homicide in Thirteenth-Century England*, Stanford University Press (1977).
7   Quoted in Power, Eileen, *The Wool Trade in English Medieval History*, Oxford University Press (1941), p. 27.

8   Jeffrey, David Lyle, *A Dictionary of Biblical Tradition in English Literature*, Wm. B. Eerdmans Publishing, (1992), p. 710.

9   *Encyclopaedia Judaica*, The Gale Group (2008).

10   Varro, M. T., *De Re Rustica* II, *Delphi Complete Works of Varro* (Illustrated), Delphi Classics (2017).

11   Longstaffe, Moya, *Joan of Arc and 'The Great Pity of the Land of France'*, Amberley Publishing (2019).

12   T., 'Critical Comments on the Bo-Peepeid: An Epic-Pastoral Poem in Three Parts', in *Monthly Literary Recreations*, Vol. 1, No. 2 (Aug. 1806).

13   Salzman, Louis Francis, *English Industries of the Middle Ages*, Library of Alexandria (2017), p. 188.

14   Opie, Iona and Opie, Peter, *The Oxford Dictionary of Nursery Rhymes*, Oxford University Press (1997), p. 108.

Chapter Seven: Dogs and Drovers

1   Horard-Herbin, Marie-Pierre, Tresset, Anne, and Vigne, Jean-Denis, 'Domestication and uses of the dog in western Europe from the Paleolithic to the Iron Age', in *Animal Frontiers*, Vol. 4, No. 3 (July 2014).

2   McKeon, Richard (ed.), with an introduction by C. D. C. Reeve, *The Basic Works of Aristotle*, Random House (2009).

3   Caius, John, *Of Englishe dogges* (1576).

4   Stilo, Aelius, *Dogs in Ancient Greece and Rome*, https://penelope.uchicago.edu/~grout/encyclopaedia_romana/miscellanea/canes/canes.html

5   Ryder, M. L., *Sheep and Man*, Gerald Duckworth and Co. Ltd (1983).

6   Parker, Heidi G., Dreger, Dayna L., Rimbault, Maud, Davis, Brian W., Mullen, Alexandra B., Carpintero-Ramirez, Gretchen, and Ostrander, Elaine A., 'Genomic Analyses Reveal the Influence of Geographic Origin, Migration, and Hybridization on Modern Dog Breed Development,' in *Cell Reports*, Vol. 19, No. 4 (2017).

7   Carroll, C. W., and Wilson, L. H., *Medieval Shepherd: Jean de Brie's Le Bon Berger 1379*, Arizona Center for Medieval & Renaissance Studies at Arizona State University (2012).

8   Ellis, William, *A Compleat System of Experienced Improvements*,

Made on Sheep, Grass-lambs, and House-lambs: Or, the Country-gentleman's, the Grazier's, the Sheep-dealer's, and the Shepherd's Sure Guide (1749).

9   Harrison, William, 'Description Of Elizabethan England', from *Holinshed's Chronicles* (1577).

10   Godwin, Fay, and Toulson, Shirley, *The Drovers' Roads of Wales*, Wildwood House Ltd (1977).

11   Russell Mitford, Mary, *Our Village*, reprinted by CreateSpace Independent Publishing Platform (2017), p. 95.

12   Skeel, Caroline, 'The Cattle Trade between Wales and England from the Fifteenth to the Nineteenth Centuries', in *Transactions of the Royal Historical Society*, Vol. 9 (1926).

13   Godwin, Fay, and Toulson, Shirley, *The Drovers' Roads of Wales*, Wildwood House Ltd (1977).

14   'Farm Ranch and Garden Department' in *The Seattle Daily Times* (21 May 1921), quoted in https://wordhistories.net/2019/08/30/judas-sheep-judas-goat/

15   Stenton, F. M., 'The Road System of Medieval England', in *The Economic History Review*, Vol. 7, No. 1 (Nov. 1936).

16   Pearlman, Jonathan, 'Australia's last cowboys: "We're not fighting to keep an old profession alive – we're fighting for our livelihood"', *The Telegraph* (26 Mar. 2017).

17   City of London, 'History of Smithfield Market' (2012), www.cityoflondon.gov.uk/business/wholesale-food-markets/smithfield/Pages/History-of-Smithfield-Market.aspx

18   Wynter, Dr Andrew, 'The London Commissariat', in *Quarterly Review*, No. cxc, Vol. xcv (1854).

Chapter Eight: Scouring and Spinning

1   Osbaldeston, Tess Anne (transl.), *The Herbal of Dioscorides the Greek*, Ibidis Press (2000).

2   Sweet, Victoria, 'Hildegard of Bingen and the Greening of Medieval Medicine', in *Bulletin of the History of Medicine*, Vol. 73, No. 3 (Fall 1999).

3   Kissell, Mary Lois, 'Ancient Greek Yarn-Making', in *The Metropolitan Museum of Art Bulletin*, Vol. 13 (1918).

4   Ovid, 'The Transformation of Arachne into a Spider', *Metamor-*

phoses, Book VI, illustrated edition by Johann Wilhelm Bauer, translated into English under the direction of Sir Samuel Garth (1713).

5 Pantelia, Maria C., 'Spinning and Weaving: Ideas of Domestic Order in Homer', in *The American Journal of Philology*, Vol. 114, No. 4 (1993).

6 Curteis, Iris, *The 'Idle Girls' in Habitrot and Three Spinners*. See www.storyvisionsource.com/the-idle-girls-in-habitrot-and-three-spinners/

7 Kirk, Robert, *The Secret Commonwealth* (1691).

8 Price, Neil S., *The Viking Way: Religion and War in Late Iron Age Scandinavia*, Department of Archaeology and Ancient History, Uppsala University (2002).

9 Smith, Hayeur *et al.*, 'Dorset, Norse, or Thule? Technological transfers, marine mammal contamination, and AMS dating of spun yarn and textiles from the Eastern Canadian Arctic', in *Journal of Archaeological Science*, Vol. 96 (August 2018).

10 Priest-Dorman, Carolyn, *Medieval North European Spindles and Whorls*, Vassar University (2000); www.cs.vassar.edu/~capriest/spindles.html

11 Eamer, Claire, 'No Wool, No Vikings: The fleece that launched 1,000 ships', *Hakai Magazine*: www.hakaimagazine.com/features/no-wool-no-vikings/

12 Ibid.

13 Postan, M. M. (ed) and Miller, E. (ed) *The Cambridge Economic History of Europe: Trade and Industry in the Middle Ages, Volume 2*, Cambridge University Press (1989), p. 625.

Chapter Nine: Knit for Victory

1 Norbury, James, 'The Knitter's Craft', in *Journal of the Royal Society of Arts*, Vol. 99, No. 4839 (26 Jan. 1951).

2 Victoria and Albert Museum, 'Regional Knitting in the British Isles & Ireland', www.vam.ac.uk/content/articles/r/regional-knitting-in-the-british-isles-and-ireland/

3 *Jackson's Oxford Journal*, Saturday, January 10th, 1852, p. 2.

4 Victoria and Albert Museum, 'The history of hand-knitting', www.vam.ac.uk/articles/the-history-of-hand-knitting

5   Letter written to the Editor by T.H., *The British Friend*, Volume 5, 1847, p. 162.

6   Altick, Richard D., *The English Common Reader: A Social History of the Mass Reading Public, 1800–1900*, University of Chicago Press (1957).

7   Mitchell, Hannah, *The Hard Way Up*, Endeavour Media (2015).

8   Ouellette, Susan M., 'All hands are enjoined to spin: textile production in seventeenth-century Massachusetts' (1996). Doctoral Dissertations 1996–February 2014. https://scholarworks.umass.edu/dissertations_1/1224

9   Smith, Adam, *An Inquiry Into the Nature and Causes of the Wealth of Nations, Volume 2*, Oliphant, Waugh & Innes (1814), p. 513.

10 'Wool and Manufactures of Wool: Special Report Relating to the Imports and Exports of Wool and Its Manufactures in the United States and the Principal Foreign Countries; United States' Department of the Treasury. Bureau of Statistics U.S. Government Printing Office (1887).

11 Stevenson, Chris, 'How Sheep Helped Start a Revolution' (11 Apr. 2016). See https://chrisstevensonauthor.com/2016/04/11/how-sheep-helped-start-a-revolution/

12 Ouellette, S. M., *Textile production in seventeenth-century Massachusetts*, University of Massachusetts (1996).

13 ifarm, 'A Stitch in Time: The Women Who Knit Together the American Revolution', https://ifarmboxford.com/stitch-time-women-knit-american-revolution/

14 Rutter, Esther, *This Golden Fleece: A Journey Through Britain's Knitted History*, Granta (2019).

15 As quoted in Field, Michael, 'Pippa's astonishing story recognised', *Stuff* (25 Nov. 2014). See www.stuff.co.nz/national/63516307/pippas-astonishing-story-recognised

16 Archival Moments, 'More than a pair of socks', http://archivalmoments.ca/2014/07/04/more-than-a-pair-of-socks/

17 Letter received by Audrey J. Reid, as published in the Digital Kingston online article 'Knitting for Soldiers', www.digitalkingston.ca/wwi-in-kingston-frontenac/knitting-for-soldiers

18 Macdonald, Anne L., *No Idle Hands: The Social History of American Knitting*, Ballantine Books (1988).

19   Burgess, Anika, *The Wool Brigades of World War I: When Knitting was a Patriotic Duty*, Atlas Obscura (2017): www.atlasobscura.com/articles/when-knitting-was-a-patriotic-duty-wwi-homefront-wool-brigades

20   Strawn, Susan M., *Knitting America: A Glorious Heritage from Warm Socks to High Art*, Voyageur Press (2011) p. 141.

21   'Knit Your Bit: The National WWII Museum provides warm gifts to Veterans', National Museum World War II Museum New Orleans, www.nationalww2museum.org/media/press-releases/knit-your-bit-national-wwii-museum-provides-warm-gifts-veterans

22   'Home Knitting Defended', *The New York Times* (22 Jan. 1942).

Chapter Ten: 'Sheepe Hath Payed For It All'

1   Fryde, E. B., 'The Last Trials of Sir William de la Pole', in *The Economic History Review New Series*, Vol. 15, No. 1 (1962).

2   Ryder, M. L., 'The History of Sheep Breeds in Britain', in *The Agricultural History Review*, Vol. 12, No. 1 (1964).

3   Grant of King Wihtred of Kent (d. 725) to St Mary's Church, Lyminge, British Library, www.bl.uk/manuscripts/FullDisplay.aspx?ref=Cotton_MS_Augustus_II_88

4   St Clair, Kassia *The Golden Thread: How Fabric Changed History*, Hachette (2018).

5   Power, Eileen, *The Wool Trade in English Medieval History*, Oxford University Press (1941).

6   Rose, Susan, *The Wealth of England: The Medieval Wool Trade and Its Political Importance 1100–1600*, Oxbow Books (2017).

7   Based on population estimates by Urlanis, B. Ts., *Rost naseleniia v Evrope: opyt ischisleniia* [*Population growth in Europe*], Moskva: OGIZ-Gospolitizdat (1941).

8   Bell, Adrian R. *et al.*, 'Advance Contracts for the Sale of Wool in Medieval England: An Undeveloped and Inefficient Market?', ISMA Centre Discussion Papers in Finance DP2005-01 (February 2005). See https://pdfs.semanticscholar.org/d1fc/274185483a02edd7aac55ff72dd703129def.pdf

9   Walter Daniel, *Vita Ailredi Abbatis Rievall*. Ed. and transl. Maurice Powicke, Oxford: Clarendon Press (1950).

10   Bell, Adrian R. *et al.*, 'Interest Rates and Efficiency in Medieval Wool Forward Contracts', *University of Reading Journal of Banking and Finance*, 31.2 (2007).

11   Jamroziak, E. M., 'Rievaulx abbey as a wool producer in the late thirteenth century: Cistercians, sheep and big debts', in *Northern History*, Vol. 40, No. 2 (2003).

12   Power, Eileen, *The Wool Trade in English Medieval History*, Oxford University Press (1941), p. 15.

13   Ibid. p. 16.

14   Postan, M. M., *Medieval Trade and Finance*, Cambridge University Press (1973), p. 342.

15   Owens, Margaret E., *Stages of Dismemberment: The Fragmented Body in Late Medieval and Early Modern Drama*, University of Delaware Press (2005), p. 178.

16   Clark, G. N., 'Trading with the Enemy and the Corunna Packets, 1689–97', in *The English Historical Review*, Vol. XXXVI, No. CXLIV (October 1921).

17   Smith, Graham, *Something to Declare: 1000 Years of Customs and Excise*, Chambers Harrap Publishers (1980).

18   Warrant Books: May 1715, 11–20 from Calendar of Treasury Books, Volume 29, 1714–1715. Originally published by Her Majesty's Stationery Office, London (1957), www.british-history. ac.uk/cal-treasury-books/vol29/pp517-52

19   Rose, Susan, *The Wealth of England: The Medieval Wool Trade and Its Political Importance 1100-1600*, Chapter 4, Oxbow Books (2017).

20   Ibid.

21   Davidson Cragoe, C, Jurica, A. R. J., and Williamson, E. A., *History of the County of Gloucester: Volume 9, Bradley Hundred. The Northleach Area of the Cotswolds*, Victoria County History, London, (2001).

22   England's Immigrants 1330–1550: Resident Aliens in the Late Middle Ages: www.englandsimmigrants.com, University of York, The National Archives and the Humanities Research Institute, University of Sheffield.

23   Delany, Sheila, *Impolitic Bodies: Poetry, Saints, and Society in Fifteenth-century England*, Oxford University Press (1998).

24   Brown, Cornelius, *History of Newark-on-Trent; being the life story of an ancient town Volume I*, S. Whiles (1904), p. 186.

Chapter Eleven: Sheep Devour People

1   Manship, Henry, *The History of Great Yarmouth*, Volume 1, Palmer, C.J. (ed.), Great Yarmouth: Louis Alfred Meall (1854).
2   Reilly, S. A., *Our Legal Heritage*, Echo Library (2007), p. 145.
3   Letter to William Spring, September 1643, as quoted in Ratcliffe, S. (Ed.), *Oxford Essential Quotations* (5th ed.), Oxford University Press (2017).
4   Stone, David, 'The Productivity and Management of Sheep in Late Medieval England', in *The Agricultural History Review*, Vol. 51, No. 1 (2003).
5   The National Archives, 'Landscape', www.nationalarchives.gov. uk/domesday/world-of-domesday/landscape.htm
6   Nicholls, Sir George, *A History of the English Poor Law, Volume 1*, Routledge (2016), p. 116.
7   Judges, A. V. (ed.), *The Elizabethan Underworld - A Collection of Tudor and Early Stuart Tracts and Ballads* (1930), p. xxxiv.
8   Green, Dr Matthew, 'A Grim And Gruesome History of Public Shaming in London: Part 2', Londonist, https://londonist.com/ 2015/12/a-history-of-public-shaming-in-london-part-2
9   More, Thomas, *Utopia*, Dover Publications Inc. (1998).
10 Shakespeare Documented, 'Thomas Greene's notes on the progress of the proposed enclosures at Welcombe include five references to William Shakespeare's involvement', https:// shakespearedocumented.folger.edu/exhibition/document/ thomas-greene-s-notes-progress-proposed-enclosures-welcombe-include-five
11 Given-Wilson, Christopher, *An Illustrated History of Late Medieval England*, Manchester University Press (1996), p. 46.
12 Prebble, John, *The Highland Clearances*, Penguin (1982), p. 79.
13 Ibid., p. 82.
14 Ascherson, Neal, *Stone Voices: The Search For Scotland*, Granta (2014).
15 Purves, Libby, *One Summer's Grace*, Chapter 20, Hachette UK (2010).
16 Quoted in Stewart, Jr., James A., 'The Jaws of Sheep: The 1851 Hebridean Clearances of Gordon of Cluny', in *Proceedings of the Harvard Celtic Colloquium*, Vol. 18/19 (1998/1999).

17 Hunter, James, 'Sheep and deer: Highland sheep farming, 1850–
    1900', in *Northern Scotland* Volume 1 (First Series), Issue 1, 1972–
    73, Edinburgh University Press, pp. 199–222.

18 G. Malcolm, 'Deer Forests: Past, Present, and Future', *Nineteenth
    Century Magazine*, 21 (1887), 691.

19 Hunter, James, 'Sheep and deer: Highland sheep farming, 1850–
    1900', in *Northern Scotland* Volume 1 (First Series), Issue 1, 1972–
    73, Edinburgh University Press, pp. 199–222.

Chapter Twelve: Spinning a Yarn

1   Heaney, Seamus, 'The Evening Land', as published in *The Aran
    Islands: At the Edge of the World*, by the Curriculum Development
    Unit, The O'Brien Press Ltd (2017).

2   Carden, Siún, 'Cable Crossings: The Aran Jumper as Myth and
    Merchandise', in *Costume*, Vol. 48, No. 2, (2014).

3   Santry, Claire, *Aran Sweaters: Truth or Fiction?*: www.irish-
    genealogy-toolkit.com/aran-sweaters.html

4   Helgadottir, Gudrun, 'Nation in a sheep's coat: The Icelandic
    sweater', in *FormAkademisk - forskningstidsskrift for design og
    designdidaktikk*, Vol. 4, No. 2 (2011).

5   Donlan, Kathleen, 'The Lopapeysa: A Vehicle to Explore the Per-
    formance of Icelandic National Identity' (2016). Honors Thesis
    Collection. 335. https://repository.wellesley.edu/thesiscollection/
    335

6   Diodorus Siculus, *Library of History*, Book V, published in Vol. III
    of the Loeb Classical Library edition (1939).

7   'Tartan and the Dress Act of 1746', Scottish Tartans Authority:
    www.tartansauthority.com/resources/archives/the-archives/
    scobie/tartan-and-the-dress-act-of-1746/

8   Scott, Walter, 'Hints Adressed to the Inhabitants of Edinburgh,
    and others, in Prospect of His Majesty's visit. By an Old Citizen',
    Printed pamphlet, Edinburgh: William Blackwood, Waugh and
    Innes, and John Robertson (1822).

9   Grant, Elizabeth, *Memoirs of a Highland Lady, the autobiography
    of Elizabeth Grant of Rothiemurchus afterwards Mrs Smith of Balti-
    boys 1797-1830*, edited by Lady Strachey, John Murray (1911),
    p. 369.

10   Scott, letter of 19 Nov. 1829 to Sir Thomas Dick Lauder, quoted in William Stewart, D., *Old and Rare Scottish Tartans*, George P. Johnston (1893).

11   Quoted in Hobsbawm, Eric, and Ranger, Terence, *The Invention of Tradition*, Cambridge University Press (1992), p. 40.

Chapter Thirteen: Mills and Boom

1   Schuman, Michael, 'History of child labor in the United States – part 1: little children working', in *Monthly Labor Review*, U.S. Bureau of Labor Statistics (January 2017).

2   Gregory, Derek, *Regional Transformation and Industrial Revolution*, Palgrave (1982).

3   Defoe, Daniel, *A Plan of the English Commerce [...] The third edition* (1749).

4   Quoted in Black, Sandy, *Knitting: Fashion, Industry, Craft* (2012), p. 19.

5   Quoted in Peyton, Jane, *Brilliant Britain: A Celebration of its Unique Traditions and Customs*, Summersdale Publishers (2012), p. 78.

6   Defoe, Daniel, *A Tour Thro' the Whole Island of Great Britain, Volume 3* (1727).

7   Stuart, John, 'The Halifax Piece Hall', in *The Yorkshire Journal*, Vol. 1 (2018).

8   Defoe, Daniel, *op. cit.* (1727).

9   Plumridge, Andrew, *The Halifax Gibbet*, Guillotine Headquarters https://guillotine.dk/pages/gibbet.html (2019).

10   Ashton, T. S., *The Industrial Revolution 1760-1830*, Oxford University Press (1968).

11   Jordan, Don, *White Cargo: The Forgotten History of White Slaves in America*, New York University Press (2008).

12   Williams, Eric, *Capitalism and Slavery*, University of North Carolina Press (1994), p. 11.

13   Hammond, J. L., & Barbara Hammond, B., *The Rise of Modern Industry*, Routledge, (2013), p. 197.

14   Humphries, Jane, 'Childhood and child labour in the British industrial revolution', in *The Economic History Review*, Vol. 66, No. 2 (2012).

15   Birley, J., interviewed by James Rayner Stephens in *The Ashton Chronicle*, 19 May 1849: http://adamsedu.weebly.com/uploads/2/8/4/1/28419347/document_c.pdf

16   Ibid.

17   *The Children Who Built Victorian Britain*, BBC Four (Wed. 10 August 2011).

18   Interview by Michael Sadler, House of Commons Committee on 21 May, 1832, quoted in Wing, Charles, *Evils of the Factory System: Demonstrated by Parliamentary Evidence*, Malbech:Psychology Press, (1967), p. 8.

19   Ibid.

20   Griffin, Emma, *Liberty's Dawn: A People's History of the Industrial Revolution, Chapter 3*, Yale University Press (2013).

21   Ibid.

22   Cooke Taylor, W., *Factories and the Factory System*, J. How (1844), pp. 23-4.

23   Ure, Andrew, *The Philosophy of Manufactures*, C. Knight (1835), p. 301.

24   Sallee, Shelley, *The Whiteness of Child Labor Reform*, University of Georgia Press (2004), p. 97.

25   McNabb, David E., *A Comparative History of Commerce and Industry*, Volume I, Palgrave (2015).

26   Briggs, Asa, *Victorian Cities*, University of California Press (1993), p. 144.

27   Keighley, Mark, *Wool City*, G. Whitaker & Company (2007).

Chapter Fourteen: Up, Up and Away

1   Collier, Aine, *The Humble Little Condom: A History*, Prometheus Books (2007).

2   Diamond, Jared, *Guns, Germs, and Steel: The Fates of Human Societies*, W. W. Norton & Company (1997).

3   Khan, Fahd *et al.*, 'The Story of the Condom', in *Indian Journal of Urology*, Vol. 29, No. 1 (2013).

4   Lynn, Michael R., *The Sublime Invention: Ballooning in Europe, 1783-1820*, Routledge (2015).

5   Ibid.

6   Lee, Tim, 'How a Cold War scientist escaped a gulag to pioneer

reproductive technology using sheep semen', *ABC News* (15 Mar. 2019). See www.abc.net.au/news/2019-03-16/cold-war-scientist-50-year-old-sheep-semen/10893706

7   Kendrick, K. M., *et al.*, 'Sheep don't forget a face', in *Nature*, Vol. 414 (2001).

8   Lee, Caroline, *et al.*, 'Development of a maze test and its application to assess spatial learning and memory in Merino sheep', in *Applied Animal Behaviour Science*, Vol. 96, No. 1 (2006).

9   Pellegrino, Nicky, 'Raising the baa', *New Zealand Listener* (22 Oct. 2015). See www.noted.co.nz/health/health-health/raising-the-baa

10 Roselli, C. E., *et al.*, 'The Volume of a Sexually Dimorphic Nucleus in the Ovine Medial Preoptic Area/Anterior Hypothalamus Varies with Sexual Partner Preference', in *Endocrinology*, Vol. 145, No. 2 (2004).

INDEX

Ackworth School, Yorkshire
156-7
Act of Union (1707) 210
Aesop's Fables 80
Aethelbald of Mercia, King 187
Akkadian culture, mythology
in 41
Alcott, Louisa May 164-5
Allen, John and Charles 236
Allet, John 250-1
America
child labour 239, 247-8, 254-5
the Great Depression 216-17
the importation of sheep 14
knitting 160-6, 171-2
displacement of the Navajo
215-17
wool production 162-3, 214
American Civil War (1861-5)
164-5
American Revolutionary War
(1775-83) 160, 163-4, 165
Amundsen, Roald 130
anthrax 258-60
Aran: Islands of Legend
(Ó Síochán) 226

Aran sweaters 224-8
Arcadia (poem) 104
Aristotle 110, 121
Arjan Tomb, the 29
Arkwright, Richard 246
art, shepherdesses in 103
artificial insemination 271
Arts and Crafts Movement 96,
229
Asiatic mouflons 4
Asikli Hoyuk, Turkey 5-6
Assyrians, the 110
astrology 73-5
Augustus, Emperor 51
Austin, Herbert 45
Australia
'Chris' (Merino sheep) 44
drove roads 123-4
knitting 172-3
science 270-1, 272
shearing 44-5
wool production 214

Babylonian culture
astrology 74-5
mythology 41

balaclavas 168
ballooning *see* hot-air
    ballooning
Balmoral Castle 236
banks 119
Barbados Blackbelly 46
bardocucullus (Roman cloak) 51
Barrett Browning, Elizabeth 252
Bedouins 54
beggars 204–7
bellwethers 9, 120–2
Bentley, Elizabeth 166
berets 25, 27–9
Bible, The 80, 99–101, 205
Birley, John 249–50
birrus (Roman garment) 50
Black Death, the 91, 197–8
Black Panthers 29
black sheep 69–73
Blake, William 98
blankets 153, 161, 168
bloat 96–8
blood transfusions 269
body armour 26, 132
bog bodies 61–4
Bon Berger, Le (de Brie) 113–14
Bonnie Prince Charlie 232
boots 25
Bowler, Mary 155–6
Bradford, England 256–8
Brahan Seer, the 214–15
breeding, trait selection 10
breeds
    Asiatic mouflon 4
    Barbados Blackbelly 46
    black sheep 69–73
    Churros 14, 215–17
    Cotswold 184

Dorset Horn 88
European Mouflon 13
Exlana 46
Hebridean 13, 146
Herdwick 10, 146
Icelandic 13
Lincoln 184
Manx Loaghtan 146
Merino 12, 43–4, 46, 88, 122,
    184, 271
Nordic 13
Norwegian Spælsau 146
Orkney 13
Ouessant 12, 146
Scottish Blackface 88
Shetlands 37
Soay 13, 37, 49, 146, 178
Southdown 88
St Croix 46
Swedish Gute 146
Bride of Lammermoor, The (Scott)
    233
Brie, Jean de 113
Britain
    the Black Death 197–8
    the Celts 49–54, 56–64,
        230–1
    child labour 247–54
    the cloth industry 247–55
    drove roads 115–22
    enclosure 200–4, 207–13
    espionage in 166–7
    exporting wool 161–3, 239
    fishing communities 222–7
    folklore 137, 138
    Highland Clearances 209–15
    importing wool 172–3, 214
    knitting 151, 152–60, 168–71

language in 68–72, 76–9,
81–3, 136, 138, 155, 179, 185
markets 116, 124–6
nålebinding 151
new breeds of sheep 46
poor relief 204–7
population growth 256
science 269–70, 273
sheepdogs 114
shepherds 91–9, 104–6
smuggling 187–90, 198
spinning 134–5
superstitions 72
textile production in 240–60
wool trade in medieval
England 177–93
British army 28–9
trench coats 130
British Journal of Nursing 168–9
broadcloth 246
buildings, sheep buried under 58
Burberry, Thomas 129–30
Burford 192
Burial in Wool Acts (1666–80)
241
Burma 8
butter 53

Cade, Jack 202
Caius, John 111
Canterbury Tales (Chaucer) 135
capes 62–3
Cappers Act (1571) 241
caps 25, 27–9, 153
carpets 21, 50
Carson, Kit 216
Casanova 266
cashmere 36

Castro, Fidel 29
'Cathedral of the Cotswolds'
(Northleach) 191
Celts, the 49–54, 56–64
tartans 230–1
Cézanne 28
Channel Islands, the 221–3
charity schools 157
Charlemagne 178–9
Chasseurs Alpins 28
Chaucer, Geoffrey 135
cheese 13, 53, 54–6
chemicals
lactose 52–3
lanolin 129–32
chewing the cud 87
child labour 239, 247–55
China
breeding in 14
dogs in 113
felt production 25
harvesting wool 36
mythology 73–5
superstitions 39, 73
Chipping Campden 192
Chipping Norton 192
'Chris' (Australian Merino
sheep) 44
churches 190–2
Churros 14, 215–17
Cirencester 192
Clancy Brothers, the 227
Clarke, John 82–3
Clearances, the 209–15
Clement VII, Pope 183
Clement, Saint 25
cloaks 42, 51, 129–30, 178–9
cloning 269–70

Clopton, Sir John 192-3
cloth halls 242-3
clothing
  balaclavas 168
  birrus 50
  boots 25
  capes 62-3
  caps and berets 25, 27-9, 153
  cloaks 42, 51, 129-30, 178-9
  gloves 153, 168
  helmets 169
  ponchos 25
  robes 42
  scarves 62, 169
  skirts 20, 62
  smocks 94-5, 129
  socks 149, 168, 169
  stockings 153, 155, 156, 158,
    169, 221
  sweaters 168, 222-3, 224-8,
    228-9
  trench coats 130
  tunics 42
  vests 168, 173
clover, dangers of eating 97
coded messages, in knitting
  165-8
Collection of English Proverbs, A
  (Ray) 79-80
Columella 112
Combe, John 208
combing 36
condoms 263-6
Congested Districts Board 227
contraception 263-6
Controversial Tracts (Wycliffe)
  78-9
Coppergate Sock, the 150-1

Corsica 13
cosmetics 130-2
Cosmopolitan magazine 239
Costume of Yorkshire, The
  (Walker) 154
Cotswolds 178, 179, 184, 240
cottage industries 132-41,
  152-4, 162
Crane, Walter 96
Crimean War (1853-6) 159
*Critical Comments on the
  Bo-Peepeid* 105
Croatia
  Croatian expression
    involving sheep 73
  shepherds' huts 94
Crompton, Samuel 246
Cromwell, Oliver 200
Culloden, Battle of (1746) 232
Cumbria 146
custom houses 187
Cyclops, the 55-6
Cyprus 13

dame schools 157
Daniel, Walter 181
d'Arlandes, François Laurent le
  Vieux 268
David Copperfield (Dickens) 252
De Re Rustica (Columella) 112
Defoe, Daniel 116, 240, 242, 243
Denmark
  Huldremose Woman 62-4
  nålebinding 150
Denys, Jean-Baptiste 269
Dhangars, the 90
Diamond, Jared 9
Dickens, Charles 125-6, 167, 252

Diocletian, Emperor 50
Dioscorides 130-1
diseases 96-8, 258-60
Dispensarium Coloniense 131
distaffs 133, 134-6, 139
dogs 57, 109-11 *see also*
    sheepdogs
Dolly the Sheep 269-70
Domesday Book 179
Donlan, Kathleen 229
Dorset Horns 88
Doyle, Phyllis, Latour 166-7
drovers and drove roads 114-26
Dudley, Ethel M. 158
dung 52
dyes 22, 63, 143

Eclogues (Virgil) 104
education 156-8
Edward I, King 70, 190
Edward II, King 121
Edward III, King 177, 185, 187,
    240
Edward IV, King 193
Edward VI, King 206
Egypt
    harvesting wool 38
    mythology 41-2
    nålebinding 149
    sacrificial rituals 101
    superstitions 39
Eid al-Adha (Festival of
    Sacrifice) 60-1
Elizabeth I, Queen 187, 221
Elkins, Ian 44
Elles, Lieutenant General Sir
    Hugh 28
Ellis, William 114

enclosure 200-4, 207-13
English Huswife, The (Markham)
    134
espionage 165-8
Eurich, Dr Friederich 258
European Mouflons 13
Evans, Jane 120
Exlanas 46
expressions and phrases
    involving sheep 67, 70, 72-3,
    76-7, 78-81, 155

fairies 138-9
fairy tales 137
Far from the Madding Crowd
    (Hardy) 97-8
Faraday, Michael 266
Farmer's Magazine, The 124-5
Fates, the 38, 136, 138, 139
felt 20, 21, 24-31
Fertile Crescent, the 4, 12, 14, 36
fishing communities 222-8
fishing lines and nets 145, 150
Flemish weavers 240
flocks 6, 9, 12, 13, 16, 44, 71, 72,
    90, 91, 92, 94, 97, 101, 102,
    152, 275
    and artificial insemination
        271
    and bellwethers 118
    and the Celts 51
    and drovers 115, 117, 120, 124
    flocking together 87-8
    in ancient Greece 43, 56
    hefted flocks 10
    homosexuality in 273
    and Little Bo-Peep 104
    in Madrid 123

in Mongolia 111
and the Navajo, in the USA
216
as religious metaphor 99
at Rievaulx Abbey 183
in Roman times 40, 178
and sheepdogs 114, 117–18,
120
on St Kilda 49
folding 92–3
folk remedies 96
folklore 137–9
foodstuffs
butter 53
cheese 13, 53, 54–6
meat 13, 49–50, 145
milk 13, 52
yoghurt 53
Fortey, John 191
foundation offerings 58
foxes 11
Fracastoro, Girolamo 265
France
espionage in 166
felt production in 28
French expressions involving
sheep 73, 80
knitting 152, 167–8
origins of Roquefort cheese
55
science 258–60, 266–8, 269
shepherds' huts 94
superstitions 71–2, 73
wool production in 132
fulling mills 160

gabardine 129–30
Galway Bay Products 226

Gammer Gurton's Garland
(Ritson) 105
ganseys 222–3
Garments and Hospital Comforts
for Our Soldiers and Sailors 169
Gaskell, Elizabeth 95, 252
Gates, Daniel 188–9
George II, King 232
George IV, King 233, 234
Georgics (Virgil) 104
Germany
and the Bradford wool trade
257
folklore 137
German expression involving
sheep 72
gloves 153, 168
gold extraction 40
Gospelles of Dystaues 71–2
Gower, John 198–9
grazing 87
Great Britain see Britain
Great Depression, the 216–17
Greece
dogs in 110
felt production 25, 26–7
mythology 55–6, 136
sacrificial rituals 101
spinning 133
wool production 132
Greenaway, Kate 96
Greene, Thomas 208
Greenland
dogs in 113
spinning and weaving 140
Guernsey 221–3
Guevara, Che 29
guilds, knitting 151–2

Halifax Gibbet 243-4
Halifax Piece Hall 242-3
Hall, Joseph 186
hand-knitting guilds 151-2
hangings 81-3
Hardy, Thomas 97-8
Hargreaves, James 246
Harrison, William 115
Harris's List of Covent Garden Ladies 263
Harsnet, Hugh 188-9
haruspex 58
Heaney, Seamus 224
Hebergam, Joseph (child mill-worker) 251
Hebridean breed 13, 146
hefting 10
helmets 169
Henry VIII, King 152, 183
herding 42-3
Herdwicks 10, 146
Herodotus 29-30
Higham, James 45
Highland Clearances 209-15
Highland Clearances, The (Prebble) 211
History of Animals (Aristotle) 110
HIV 266
Hobsbawm, Eric 229-30
Homer 55-6, 136
homosexuality in sheep 273-4
horns 10-11
horses 57
hot-air ballooning 266-8
Huldremose Woman 62-4
Humphries, Professor Jane 250

'Ice Maiden,' the 20-1
Iceland 13
   dogs in 113
   Icelandic expression involving sheep 73
   Icelandic sweater (*lopapeysa*) 228-9
   spinning and weaving 140
immigration 192
Incas, mythology 137
India
   felt production 25
   shepherds in 90
Industrial Revolution 95, 209, 246-60
intelligence, sheep 272-3
Intergovernmental Panel of Climate Change (UN) 276
Inuit peoples 141
Invention of Tradition 225-36
Iran
   Arjan Tomb 29
   discovery of woollen textiles 15
Iraq 16
Ireland 224-8
Isle of Man 60, 146
Italy
   dogs in 113
   felt production 26, 27, 28
   Italian expressions involving sheep 73, 80
   sacrificial rituals 101
   shepherds' huts 94
   superstitions 72
   wool production 132
   wool trading and banking 182-3

Jack Cade's Rebellion (1450) 202

Jacobite Revolts 210, 232, 233

James II, King (of England) 232

James V, King (of Scotland) 232

James VII, King (of Scotland) see James II

Japan 74

Jason and the Golden Fleece 39–40, 41

Johnson, John de Monins 149

Jones, Sir Horace 126

Jordan 6

jumpers see sweaters

Kay, John 246

Kelly, Grace 227

Kett's Rebellion (1549) 202

Khan, Genghis 30

Khnum (Egyptian god) 41

King Lear (Shakespeare) 134–5, 208

Kingsley, Charles 252

Kirk, Robert 138

Kissell, Mary Lois 42–3

'Knit for Victory' campaigns 168–74

Knitters' Guild, Paris 152

knitting 22, 151–74
    Knitting for Infants and Juniors (Dudley) 158
    knitting machinery 154

knives, for shearing 36

lactose 52–3

Lake District 10, 146

lambs, weaning 7–8

Landsteiner, Karl 269

language, sheep influences 67–83, 136, 138, 150, 155, 179, 185

lanolin 129–32

Laurence of Ludlow 189–90

Lavenham 192

Levengle, Madame 166

Lightfoot, Amy 144

Lincoln sheep 184

literature, shepherding in 97–101, 103–4

Little Women (Alcott) 164–5

livestock guardians 110–12

Lloyd, Robert 119

Lombe, Thomas 246

Long Melford 192

lookers 91–2

lopapeysa (Icelandic sweater) 228–9

Louis XVI, King 267–8

Luttrell Psalter 94

MacDonald, Grace 211–12

machinery 154, 246–7

Mackenzie, Alexander 214–15

Magdalene Laundries scandal 227–8

Mainwaring, Arthur 208

Makem, Tommy 227

makkin belt 153

Manx Loaghtans 146

Marie Antoinette 267

markets 116, 124–6

Markham, Gervase 134

Marlowe, Christopher 104

Mary, Queen of Scots 221

mattresses 25

Mauroy, Antoine 269

McMaister, John 212
McQueen, Steve 227
Measure for Measure
(Shakespeare) 76–7
meat 13, 49–50, 145
Meckenem, Israhel van 135
Medici family 182–3
medicinal properties of lanolin
130–1
Merinos 12, 43–4, 46, 88, 122,
184, 271
Mesopotamia 36, 101
metal shears 36–9
Metropolitan Museum of Art 42
Midland Revolt (1607) 203
milk 13, 52
Minoan culture 27
Mitchell, Anthony 244
Mitchell, Hannah 158
Mitford, Mary Russell 117–18
monasteries 179, 180–2, 183,
204
Monet 28
Mongol Empire 30–2
Mongolia
breeding in 14
deadly disease afflicts sheep
in 31
livestock guardians 111
shepherds 90
Monroe, Marilyn 227
Montgolfier brothers 266–8
Montgomery, Sir John 193
More, Thomas 207
Morrison, Sophia 60
Morton, Jenny 273
moulting 35
mummification 41

mutton 49–50
mythology
the Fates 38, 136, 138, 139
Jason and the Golden Fleece
39–40, 41
Mama Ocllo 137
the mummification of sheep
41
Odysseus and the Cyclops
55–6
the origins of Roquefort 55
seidr (Viking magic) 139
'Spider Woman' (in Navajo
culture) 136–7
the Three Norns 138, 139
the zodiac 73–5

nålebinding 149–51
*National Society's Instructions
on Needlework and Knitting,
The* 158
Natural History (Pliny) 53
Navajo culture 215–17
mythology 136–7
Navajo Sheep Project 217
Nepal 36
New Guinea 7–8
New Zealand
'Shrek' (Merino sheep) 44
wool production 214
Newfoundland 141
Noah's Ark 25
Noftall, Edward 169–70
nomads 19–22, 25–6, 29–30, 31,
89–90
Nordic sheep breeds 13
North and South (Gaskell) 95
Northleach 192

Norway 64, 113, 144, 150, 197
    Norwegian Spælsau 146
nursery rhymes 69–71, 104–6

Ó Síochán, Pádraig 226
Odysseus 55–6
Odyssey (Homer) 55–6
Offa, King of Mercia 178–9
Oliver Twist (Dickens) 125–6
Orczy, Baroness 167–8
Orkney 72, 78
    breed of sheep 13, 146
orphanages 155
Ouessant breed 12, 146
outworkers 241, 244–5
Ovid 133–4
owling (sheep smuggling) 187–9

Pakistan 39
parachutes 268
*Passionate Shepherd to His Love,
    The* (poem) 104
Pasteur, Louis 259–60
Pazyryk (nomads) 19–22, 24,
    25
Peasants' Revolt (1381) 202
Periegetes, Dionysius 178
pets, sheep as 7–8
Phillip, Captain Arthur 44
phrases involving sheep 67, 70,
    72–3, 76–7, 78–81, 155
Picasso, Pablo 28
piece work 241, 244–5
pigs 57
Pilgrim Fathers, the 161
Pitt the Younger, William 248
place names, sheep-related
    77–8, 179

Plato 136
Pliny 26, 51, 53
plucking 36
Plutarch 80–1
Pole, John de la 177
Pole, William de la 177
Polo, Marco 30
Polosmak, Natalia 19–20
ponchos 25
poor relief 204–7
Potter, Beatrix 10
Prebble, John 211
proverbs, sheep-related 79–81
putting out (production system)
    241, 244–5

Quaker schools 156–7

Ranger, Terence 229–30
Ray, John 79–80, 81
Red Cross, the 171
religious orders 179–80, 183,
    204
religious schools 156–7
Rembrandt 28
remedies 130–1
rennet 54
Republic (Plato) 136
Reynolds, John 203–4
rhymes 69–71, 104–6
Richard I, King 179
Richard III, King 177
Riders to the Sea (Synge)
    225–6
Rinker, Molly 'Old Mom' 165
Ritson, Joseph 105
Rob Roy (Scott) 233
robes 42

Rome, ancient 40, 49, 51, 61,
101, 102, 111, 200, 230
birrus 50
use of felt by Roman army
26-7
and lanolin 132
livestock guardian dogs 110,
114
mythology 38, 136, 138, 139
Roman writers on sheep's
milk 53
ovine contraception 263
Romans establish a wool
industry in Britain 177-8
shears 36
sheep entrails used for
divination in 57-8
and sheep's cheese 54
and spinning 133, 136, 139
and tartan 231
wool production 132
rooing 36
rope 145
Roslin Institute, Scotland
269-70
Rouse, Richard 124
Rozier, Jean-François Pilâtre
de 268
Russia 11, 14, 19, 150
espionage in 166
folklore 137-8
Pazyryk nomads 19-22, 24,
25

sacrificial rituals 57-64, 100-1
*Sacrificial Customs and other
Superstitions in the Isle of Man*
(Morrison) 60

sails 142-4
Salamon, Dr Steven 270-1
Sannazaro, Jacopo 104
Sardinia 13
shepherds' huts 94
sayings 67, 70, 72-3, 76-7,
78-81, 155
Sayings of Saint Bernard, The 79
Scarlet Pimpernel, The (Orczy)
167-8
scarves 62, 169
schools 156-8
science
anthrax vaccination 258-60
artificial insemination 271
blood transfusions 269
cloning 269-70
condoms 263-6
homosexuality in sheep
273-4
hot air balloons 266-8
sheep intelligence 272-3
scissors 35
Scotland 49, 68, 116, 137, 146,
269-70
Highland Clearances 209-15
National Museum of
Scotland 270
tartan 230-36
Scott, Robert 130
Scott, Walter 233-4, 235-6
Scottish Blackfaces 88
scouring 130
Scythians 21-2, 24, 29-30
searchers 186-7
Seattle Daily Times (newspaper)
120-1
seidr 139

sexually transmitted diseases
263, 265–6
Shackleton, Ernest 130
Shakespeare, William 76, 134,
207–8
shearing
combing 36
knives 36
metal shears 36–9
plucking 36
scissors 35
shearing machines 45
stone scrapers 36
sheep blast 96–8
sheep stealing 81–3
Sheep Trust, the 146
sheepcovers 43
sheepdogs 109–18
droving 117–18
herding dogs 111–14
livestock guardians 110–12
origins of 6–7
sheepskin 63
Shelley, Mary 8
*Shepherd and Shepherdess
Making Music* (tapestry) 103
Shepherd of Salisbury Plain, The
154–5
Shepherdess of the Glaciers, The
(film) 103
shepherds 42–3
folding 92–3
huts 92, 93–4
in literature 97–101
lookers 91–2
nomadic 19-22, 25–6, 29–30,
31, 89–90
qualities of 98–9

semi-nomadic 90
shepherdesses 101–6
smocks 94–5
transhumant shepherds
90–1
treating diseases 96–8
shepherds' huts 92, 93–4
shepherd's score, the 68–9
Shetlands 37
shields 26
'Shrek' (New Zealand Merino
sheep) 44
Siculus, Diodorus 231
skin creams 130–2
skirts 20, 62
Smith, Adam 161
Smithfield Market 116, 124–6
smocks 94–5, 129
smuggling 187–9, 198
Soays 13, 37, 49, 146, 178
socks 149, 168, 169
Southdowns 88
Southwold 192
Spain
drove roads 122–3
felt production 28
knitting 151
wool production 132
spinning 132–41
Spring, Sir William 200
St Croix 46
Stamford Mercury (newspaper)
82–3
Statute Concerning Diet and
Apparel (1363) 199–200
Statute of Labourers (1351) 198,
205
Stiner, Mary 5

stockings 153, 155, 156, 158, 169, 221
Stokesay Castle 189
stone scrapers, for shearing 36
Strabo 50, 51
Stuart, Charles Edward 235, 236
Stuart, John Sobieski 235, 236
Suetonius 27
Sumerian culture 41
sumptuary laws 199
superstitions 39, 71-3
sustainability 275-7
Sustainable Food Trust 276
Sverre, King (of Norway) 145
sweaters 168, 222-3, 224-8, 228-9
Swedish Gute 146
syphilis 265-6

Tacitus 61-2
Tale of Two Cities, A (Dickens) 167
tallow 145
Tanner, Thomas 188-9
tartans 230-6
Tatler magazine 170
tattoos 41
tax on wool 70, 187, 190, 239-40
Taylor, John 207, 243-4
Taylor, William Cooke 252-3
tents 25, 145
termination offerings 58
textile mills 160, 246-60
textiles see also wool
  broadcloth 246
  felt 20, 21, 24-31
  gabardine 129-30
  sheepskin 63

tartans 230-6
worsted 246
Thompson, E. P. 208
Thornton, Colonel 268
Three Norns, the 138, 139
Time magazine 173
Tømmervik Textile Trust, Norway 144
traditions, invention of 225-36
transhumant shepherds 90-1
trench coats 130
Tresham, Sir Thomas 203
tricoteuses 167-8
Tuddenham, Sir Thomas 193
tunics 42
Turkey 5-6
turpentine 96
Twelfth Night (Shakespeare) 134
Tyler, Wat 202
Tyrell, Sir William 193

Ulaanbaatar 31
UN Intergovernmental Panel of Climate Change 276
Ure, Andrew 253-4
USA see America
Utopia (More) 207
Uyun al-Hammam, Jordan 6

Varro (Roman writer) 40, 102
Vere, John de 193
vests 168, 173
Victoria and Albert Museum, London 151
Victoria, Queen 159-60, 236
Vietnam 74
Viking Ship Museum, Denmark 144

Vikings, the
    colonization and trade 141-6
    mythology 138, 139
    nålebinding 150-1
    spinning 139-41
Virgil 104

Wales 68, 116, 120, 236, 245
    drovers' banks in 119
Walker, George 154
Wallace, William 124
Washington, George 164
Wealth of Nations (Smith) 161
'Weaver and the Factory Maid,
    The' (song) 255
weaving 22, 137-8, 140
Weerth, George 258
Weldon's wool company 169
'white death' (disease affecting
    Mongolian sheep) 31
White Monks, the 180-1
Wihtred of Kent, King 178
Wilkinson, John 244
William III, King 162
Wilson, President 171
Wollstonecraft, Mary 8
Wolseley, Frederick York 45
wool
    archaeological finds 19-22
    becomes a valuable
        commodity 16

cashmere 36
dyes 22, 63, 143
early domesticated sheep
    13
knitting 22, 151-74
lanolin 129-32
machinery 246-7
nålebinding 149-51
properties of 22-5
selective breeding for 14-16
spinning 132-41
tax on 70, 187, 190, 239-40
weaving 22, 137-8, 140
wool trade in medieval
    England 177-93
Wool Act (1699) 163
wool churches 190-2
Woolsack, the 185-6
workhouses 155-6
World War I (1914-18) 130, 166,
    168-73
World War II (1939-45) 166-7,
    173-4
worsted 246
Wulff, Graham 131-2
Wycliff, John 78-9

yoghurt 53
yurts 29-32

zodiac, the 73-5

Sally Coulthard is a bestselling author of nature and outdoor living books including *The Hedgehog Handbook*, *Biophilia*, *The Bee Bible*, *The Little Book of Building Fires*, *The Little Book of Snow* and *Gardenalia*. She lives on a Yorkshire smallholding which she shares with her husband, three girls and – naturally – a small flock of sheep.